Best-Selling Author, Rocky "Rockstar" McElveen ("Wild Men, Wild Alaska") brings you this fabulous sequel! Check out "www.rockymcelveen.com" for ways to book Rocky for a Wild Game Dinner, a highly popular event for all types of audiences. Rocky is a sought after National Speaker and does Radio and TV shows in the US and Canada. You can order his books, individually signed at: "www.alaskan-adventures.com. Retail vendors or those involved in non-profit work may order this sequel from the publisher at great discounts: www.bigmacpublishers.com. If you like Rocky's books please take an extra moment to leave a review on Amazon, suggest search tags and click on those reviews that are helpful. Consider giving these books as gifts as well. Others will discover these classic stories and their life changing principles. This would be greatly appreciated by Rocky, his fans and publisher. Email Rocky with your comments and suggestions!

Tight Lines, Straight Shots!

Can't Visit the Real Alaska?
We're Bringing Alaska To You.

The very long driveway to our log cabin in Alaska. It took forever after a snowfall for me and my brothers to shovel it out so our station wagon could traverse it. I hated that driveway!

Rocky has done it again! This long awaited sequel is every bit as exciting, interesting and witty as his first best-selling book, "Wild Men, Wild Alaska." It will keep you in suspense and will put the Alaskan wilderness into your hands.

It reveals more about Rocky and the unique life he has lived. These intense tales are for the young, old, men, women, boys, girls and everything in between. These are stories of coming of age, fathers and sons, plane wrecks, grizzly confrontations, being stranded in the wild and young men and women adventurers in their quest to survive and compete in the last frontier. In so doing, they learn the rhythm of their soul. It is a book that you won't put down until you've read every last story. And then you might want to read them again!

Survival of the Fittest . . .

View from Lodge . . .

Home grown vegetables at the lodge, cabbage the size of a watermelon, broccoli the size of a basketball.

Wild Men, Wild Alaska II

The Survival of the Fittest.

Or

Action Adventure, Outdoor Life. Young Men &
Women Adventurers in their Quest to Survive.
Coming of Age in the Alaskan Wilderness.

Rocky C. McElveen

Big Mac Publishers
Riverside, California

any part of this book, except for brief quotations in critical reviews or articles.

Author: Rocky McElveen
Editor: Greg Bilbo
Cover Photo: ANWR / US Wild Fish & Wildlife Service / Steve Chase
Weasel/Caribou Photos: US Fish & Wildlife Service / Steve Hildebrand
All other Photos: Copyright © 2009   Rocky McElveen
Cover Illustration / Design: Greg Bilbo
Proofreaders: Leslie & DeeAnn William-
son

Scripture quotations are from THE NEW KING JAMES VERSION. Copyright © 1979, 1980, 1982, 1990, 1994 by Thomas Nelson, Inc.

Many of the quotations at beginning of chapters and throughout are from: http://www.chiriquichatter.net/blog/category/asides/
Some jokes and one-liners are from: "Pocket Humor" by Robert Alston
See all of Alston's books on wisdom, management, humor & leadership.

Library of Congress Control Number: 209904310
Library of Congress subject headings:
1. Adventures and Adventurers – Alaska
2. Outdoor Life – Alaska
3. Hunting – Alaska
4. Fishing – Alaska

BIASC / BASIC Classification Suggestions:
1. BIO023000 BIOGRAPHY & AUTOBIOGRAPHY / Adventurers & Explorers
2. SPO022000 SPORTS & RECREATION / Hunting
3. SPO014000 SPORTS & RECREATION / Fishing
4. BIO018000 BIOGRAPHY & AUTOBIOGRAPHY / Religious

ISBN-13: 978-0-9823554-1-1   **ISBN-10:** 0-9823554-1-6   V: 1.2
Big Mac Publisher Book Titles may be purchased in bulk at great discounts by retail vendors, or for educational, business, fund-raising, spiritual or sales promotionals. Contact info @ Big Mac Publisher's website.

Published by Big Mac Publishers
www.bigmacpublishers.com / Riverside, California 92504
Printed and bound in the United States of America

Dedication

I would like to thank my dad, Floyd McElveen, for getting off the couch and going to Alaska when it was such a formidable task. In the mid 1950's the Alaska Highway was a challenge, no McDonalds and no freeways. Dad pursued God's call and the results will resound in Heaven. He chose to expose his family to a rough, wild Alaska.

My mom, Virginia, always stood by his side for better or for worse. Was life fair? Probably not. However, their faith, their love for each other, their commitment to Christ, and incredible desire to see everyone know Jesus as their personal Savior, are still the four pillars of their life. In spite of raising a wild and sometimes reckless kid, Mom and Dad, this book is for you. Enjoy reliving the journey. Greg, Rocky, Randy and Ginger will always be blessed because of you both.

Tight Lines, Straight Shots,

Rocky "RockStar" McElveen

Big Mac Publishers

Rocky has fished and hunted with the famous and not so famous, but one thing never changes. And that is the awesome experiences they had in the great State of Alaska—unique experiences that have changed some lives forever.

And from celebrities to common folks, they all love the humor, wackiness and derring-do that we have come to know and love as Rockstar!

President Bush Sr., catching some nice salmon.

Table of Contents

"Reading is a means of thinking with another person's mind; it forces you to stretch your own." Charles Scribner, Jr.

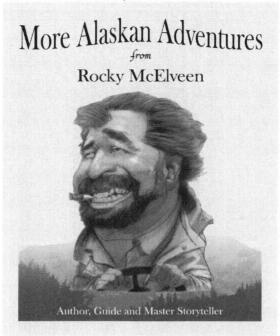

More Alaskan Adventures
from
Rocky McElveen

Author, Guide and Master Storyteller

Help! Help! This Dead Bear is trying to Eat Me!!

Another staff member bites the dust . . .

Introduction

"A guide is just a psychologist with a bigger office."

I think that on the day God got up to create Alaska, He had one too many cups of Starbucks coffee, probably an extra large "Venti" with triple espresso. Either that or He was getting a little bored with all the neat little places He had created on Earth. Maybe He just wanted to make that one place without equal, so unusually spectacular and rugged that it would likely never be fully conquered.

Otherwise, how do you explain a land that is quite simply over the top in every respect, and so beyond the pale of almost any other? A land with such an extremely harsh environment, that when it was originally purchased for $7.2 million, or about two cents per acre, it was dubbed "Seward's Folly" after the man who brokered the sale. Let me suggest that this "folly" was probably the best deal ever made. It makes the trunk of beads traded for Manhattan a virtual rip-off in comparison.

Alaska has swallowed up the brave, the foolish, the adventurer, the rich, the poor and countless missionaries. It has been home and often the final resting place to a hodge-podge of quirky people from around the globe. I think the secrets it contains and the bodies it has enveloped far exceed those of the bayous of Louisiana, the vast swamps of Florida or the sands of the Sahara combined. If you are still inclined to challenge Alaska, consider this bit of wisdom from Johnny Carson: "Don't moon a pit bull if you've been sitting in A-1 Sauce!"

The following incident, told in the chapter "A Son Stands Tall," happened to one of my guests.

His mind was reeling and Kev was berating himself under his breath, "Kev! Kev! You are so stupid! What have you done?" His son was right next to him and down on one knee. They were in a remote clearing in the Alaskan wil-

derness. Kev had dreamed for months of this father-son trip in the wilds, a chance to bond with his lad and celebrate his 14th birthday. But not like this! A huge 700-pound Alaskan grizzly was charging, and one or both of them would surely die before their puny bullets might dissuade the monstrous creature. The chance of hitting a vital spot on this oncoming hurtling mass of fur and fury was slim. They were out in the open and exposed—nowhere to run.

Kev had a crazy thought: His ex-wife would be furious that he had brought Trent up here to be killed. Huh? Why was he thinking that? Who cared about that now? This powerful, howling beast obviously didn't and was now in a full run, teeth bared, muscles rippling, claws flashing and headed straight at Kev's boy.

I grew up in Alaska. I am a long-time big-game Alaskan guide. I have learned, however, that the real story is not about big trophy game. The true story is Alaska and its incredible impact on the lives it touches. Shared adventures foster intensity in relationships and personal growth, whether love, hate, coming of age, discovering your heart, facing danger or the struggle to survive. Alaska is the barometer for the soul of adventure.

I was there before it became a state, when it was only a territory run by the military. I have nearly been buried there too, several times. I carry the marks of my journey on my body and in my heart. Let me share with you a few more of my Alaskan adventures in this sequel to my first book, *Wild Men, Wild Alaska.*

As a young boy, I remember reading Jack London's tales of the far north. Oh, the wolves were prowling; boys and men were challenging the unknown and confronting the unpredictable wilderness. Such classics as *The Call of the Wild,* by Jack London, inspired my brothers and me, and I wanted to live the things we read about. In the process, God allowed me, and countless others who shared some of my wilderness journeys, to find the true beat of our hearts. Some of us found our souls, many found soul mates but I would venture that all of us found ourselves and were better for it.

These stories are not mere accounts of awesome encounters in the wild. That is only the setting, the framework, a stage from which lives have been changed. No, these are much more. They are tales of discovery and enlightenment, pain and fear, success and failure. They are about my early adventures, about other sons and fathers, family struggles, relationships and other men and boys seeking themselves and a deeper meaning in life. Facing death, facing the cruel unleashed power of nature or facing your inner self, vulnerable and revealed, can jumpstart that process in a hurry.

I felt very blessed that men and women, young and old, loved my first book, and for many of the same reasons, I think you will enjoy this one. Speaking of the ladies, I think you will gain a much deeper understanding of how men tick and why they crave and need adventure. Especially considering that, in my experience, many wedding ceremonies probably should have begun with "In this corner . . .," you may even discover that some wilderness time confronting the wild in Alaska, instead, would be an amazing blessing for you too.

I have indeed lived similar versions of those stories London so vividly wrote about. My hope is to impact you like he influenced my brothers and me. So, without further comment, I offer you a little more of my wild Alaskan adventures. . .

Welcome to Alaska! Set your watch back 200 years.

Alaska State Map

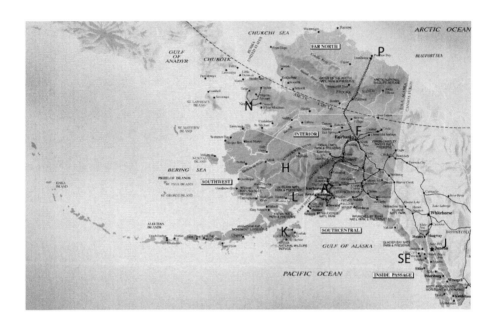

A. Anchorage (lower middle)
F. Fairbanks (upper right middle)
H. Holitna Lodge (My Lodge, Middle of Nowhere)
J. Juneau (Capital) (lower right, SE Alaska)
K. Kodiak Island (bottom middle)
L. Lake Clark (below Holitna Lodge)
N. Nome (middle left)
P. Prudhoe Bay (top right, Oil Fields)
SE. Southeast Alaska (lower right)

Chapter One

Hidden Secret of Cooper Creek

"Don't mess with Mom."

"**D**addy! Daddy!" we screamed. "Help! Help!" Our high-pitched young voices knifed through the misty morning air in blood-curdling shrieks. My brother and I were outside our log cabin in Cooper's Landing, Alaska, at about 5 a.m. We were hunched up, huddled together in the freezing cold and headed to the woodshed to get more logs for the fire. In the process, we had walked into a deadly trap.

Our one bedroom Cooper Creek log cabin. No water, lights or toilet-perfect for family of 6.

Getting wood was our daily early morning ritual, just one of many such chores each family member was given. We had no phones, electricity or running water, except when Dad would say, "Rocky, run get the water!" Our refrigerator was large and seasonal. During the winter, it was the whole outdoors.

At one point in my childhood, we lived in a one-bedroom log cabin, and our only source of heat was a wood-burning barrel stove. While others brag about a "bath and a half," we had a tub and a path. Mom would wash her feet before retiring to bed, and if she left the basin of water on the floor, it would be frozen by morning. Our discarded socks would freeze overnight and stick to the floor. Due to the cabin's humidity, the inside of the logs would develop a white frost.

Sometimes when a blizzard hit, the snow would pile up and we would have to dig our way out because the cabin doors would be sealed shut. Several times the snow was so high we had to tunnel out from a small window in the attic. The coldest temperature we ever recorded at our cabin was *minus* 35 degrees not counting wind-chill. How cold is that? Well, when people talked their words would freeze. Of course, when it thawed, the noise would be deafening! *Baby, it was cold outside.*

I have two brothers, one older, one younger, and a sister who is the youngest. My brothers and I slept in the loft. It was very cramped, and even though we were short, we could not stand upright. We used a homemade, makeshift ladder made from Alaskan black pine trees to crawl carefully up through a square hole in the ceiling.

We always put a couple of nice sized logs into the wood stove just before going to bed. The fire would burn brightly for a while, the warm heat rising, and the house and especially the loft would become nice and toasty—for about three or four hours. Then the fire would die and the chilling cold would set in. By five in the morning we'd be cold and stiff, pulling worn blankets and anything else we could find tightly around us to try to keep warm. Going outside in the icy cold to use the outhouse or fetch wood in winter was a monumentally dreaded task at any time of the day or night.

On this particular morning, we had stumbled directly between a cow moose and her young calf. Now, there is nothing more ferocious in the world than a mother that perceives a threat to her child. Something rises up inside of even the most genteel of ladies and they become monsters of invincibility. They will take on all odds to protect their young. This cow moose heard us and, when she turned to investigate, saw that we were near her precious little one. Talk about being in the wrong place at the wrong time! We may have been small, but we immediately became a big threat in her eyes.

She reared around like a horse trying to toss its rider and her hooves came up into the air. They looked like big billy clubs to us. The moment those hooves hit the snow she charged straight at us. We just stood there all bunched up, transfixed with fear, screaming uncontrollably. My eyes locked wide open and stared intently at this "locomotive" charging pell-mell, nostrils flaring, bent on saving her child.

She was coming at us like an old-fashioned steam engine, belching volumes of breath that resembled smoke coming from her mouth in the cold air. Her eyes were wide open and she was fiercely angry. She was only about 40 yards away and closing fast. Her big ears were laid back and her fur was standing straight up on the hump behind her head. I knew I was going to die. I was going to be stomped to death. I wondered how my red blood would look all over the white snow.

Although we did not hear them, screams were coming from inside the cabin too. Our mom was yelling her fool head off. Her own babies were in danger! She was sitting half up in bed, flailing her arms and shaking her head, her long, beautiful brown hair tossing wildly about. Our fear, transmitted via our voices, had roused her and chilled her to the bone. Her piercing screams propelled Dad from a sound sleep. He must have thought he was having the mother of all nightmares.

Dad flew out of his bed as if walking on air, feet barely touching the floor. Covers went flying and his faded yellow long johns were all twisted and askew. His sleep-ridden eyes were staring wildly as if he were seeing a ghost. He was trying desperately to comprehend where he was and what was happening. His bushy, black hair was bunched to one side and looked like a wave about to crash on the beach. He was crashing too, into the log walls, until our screams registered in his brain. He grabbed the first thing he saw—a thin stick of kindling wood—and sailed out the door, barefoot into the icy snow, terrified at what he would find.

Mom and Dad were not the only ones who had heard our screams. We had two beautiful, large, golden mixed Labrador-Huskies that also had been alerted. We loved those dogs. We had owned them since they were pups. The male we called King and the female, Queen. King was slightly bigger than Queen and they were inseparable. I guess I thought of them as having the perfect marriage. They fought now and then, but King was always looking after her and she kept him out of trouble.

Dad had come by a small but genuine Alaskan dog sled, and we had great fun being pulled around by the dogs using makeshift harnesses for them. Queen was one of the smartest animals I have ever known. Mom taught her a bunch of tricks, and Queen even learned how to climb a 20-foot ladder without assistance. She was amazing. I have always wondered why she, the female, was so much smarter than King, but, then again, maybe I'd better leave that question alone.

Both dogs rounded the corner of the cabin in a full gallop, snow flying, teeth bared, growling and barking like crazy. It sounded like a war zone. My brother and I were squealing and crying, the dogs were yelping and howling, the moose was snorting and belching and Mom was screaming and yelling more than all of us put together. It is a wonder the small moose calf didn't die from fright!

The cow moose was almost upon us, and I cringed in anticipation of getting walloped. (As Delilah said to Sampson, "Arise! The Philistines are upon you.") However, I was so scared I couldn't move, and my brother was just as frightened and paralyzed. I could focus on nothing else but those huge front hooves flying toward my face.

Then I saw a golden flash. The moose slid to a stop on all fours only a few feet in front of me. I saw King launch himself into the air and, using his powerful jaws, clamp for all he was worth onto the moose's snout. He dangled there in front of my unbelieving eyes as the moose began bucking and backing up, trying to shake this "yellow wolf" from her nose.

Meanwhile, Queen was diving at the back legs of the moose, biting her hindquarters and shins ferociously. All at once, the moose gave a mighty flip of her head and sent King sailing into the air like a rag doll. He landed hard on his back in the snow a good ten feet away, but pounced up immediately and charged that moose again! I stood there motionless, mouth agape, watching beast against beast. What a sight!

The poor moose had had enough. By this time, her calf had run past her, and she turned and fled with it into the woods. As far as I could see them, King and Queen were in hot pursuit right on their heels, barking ferociously, letting them know that we boys were off limits and to keep on going if they knew what was good for them. Yeah, King and Queen, you guys rock!

At that moment, it got very quiet. The adrenaline that had been flowing non-stop dissipated, and my body began shaking wildly. Almost as if on cue, my brother and I collapsed into the snow. Was it the melting snow on our pajamas that made those wet spots?

I looked over at the steps that led to the side door of the cabin from which Dad had exited. I saw Mom standing there in a wrinkled nightgown, her left hand on her hip, hair in a mess. In her right hand, she held a loaded .357 magnum handgun she kept at her bedside. I think she had gotten there just as the dogs charged the moose.

She was looking at Dad, who was standing shoeless and clueless in the snow between us and mom, still gripping that skinny piece of wood in his hand. His long johns looked as if they were going to fall off, and he appeared shell-shocked.

Mom had that bemused look on her face that she gets when she is going to say something special. I think all moms have a similar look: head slightly tilted forward, eyebrows squinched and partly raised, a small smirky smile on their lips. Mom twirled the gun around and idly swung it up and down slowly, emphatically, all the while staring pointedly at the piddling stick in Dad's hand.

My brother sensed something was up and began watching Mom too. Dad knew better than to say anything. Any man with the sense of a billy goat knows that there are certain moments when silence is truly golden and any speech is treacherous, but in spite of himself, Dad began to fidget. Maybe it was from the ice and snow getting to his bare feet, and maybe it wasn't.

Then, in that southern drawl that only Mom can do, she said, "M-a-a-a-c," drawing out his nickname derisively. She continued in a sweet voice, "Since you bolted right past all those guns in the house, sweetie, I gotta know something." Here she paused a moment for emphasis and then with some real vigor barked, "Just what were you going to do with that tiny little toothpick in your hand, dear? Were you going to clean that lady's teeth!?"

Oh, my goodness! Greg and I were astounded. I looked at Dad, who stood speechless. In unison, my brother and I burst out laughing hysterically. We were writhing in the snow, giggling and hollering until our stomachs hurt. The dogs joined in. They started jumping up and down on us, wagging their tails and licking our cheeks. Dad and Mom were laughing in concert. It was indeed a magical moment—one that I will cherish forever.

In many family discussions about this event over the years, Mom still gets tickled over our collective recollections and descriptions, and of course, Dad denies his role in it entirely.

Video games, television, computers, the Internet, dubious music, electronic gadgets, cell phones and a host of other things saturate and dominate the lives of our youth. They're accustomed to creating pseudo fantasy excitement. But nothing can compare to the bonding and personal growth that accompanies real adventures with your family.

My father came to me a few years ago. He said, "Rock, I have wanted to say this many times before and should have, but at least I am saying it now. I want to ask your forgiveness for how hard I worked you and your brothers when you were young." I was shocked and inwardly pleased, but then I thought about it. I replied simply, "Dad, there is nothing to forgive."

I have often reflected on the chores we did as kids. On the 2nd page of this book is a picture of the l-o-n-g driveway we shoveled. My parents both grew up on farms in rough times and spent much of their day doing necessary work for simple survival. We did too. I believe hard work produces character. Sometimes at speaking engagements I ask audiences how much of their kid's day is spent on such things.

I suspect that many young men and women of a bygone era spent as much as 90 percent of their available free time on chores that contributed to their family's survival, or on improving and building the family unit and home into something special. The answer I get from most modern audiences when I ask this question is that less than five percent of their children's time is spent on anything that really contributes to the family's well-being.

I truly believe that even though it was extremely difficult for my siblings and me, it was still an awesome foundation for our lives and far better than the stuff those chores and family values have been replaced with today. Children are confused about their roles. Gender roles, I feel, are best modeled by moms and dads passing along tasks for their kids to learn. I think one function of family childhood chores is that they inject a "behavioral inoculation" to combat family dysfunction. Families that work together become a unit, a team. They become functional!

For thousands of years man has lived without all those modern gadgets, and I am convinced our core values have taken a huge hit because of them. Used correctly, they are wonderful, but too often their overuse creates disconnection. Kids are connected to cell phones, computers, the Web and who knows what else. They just aren't connected to their families, to their parents or to a strong foundation of faith. I must admit that my brother and I did try to convince Dad that since that moose nearly got us killed, we should be relieved of getting firewood in the morning. I am glad to report that those pleas were to no avail.

Real Treasure

We truly lived off the land. Moose, caribou, spruce hen, berries, wild rhubarb, crab, clams, trout, salmon and our own vegetable garden provided most of our fare. Even with the gifts of wild game and homegrown garden vegetables for our table, our life was very hard and the basics of life were scarce, especially when it got really cold. We had a home-dug well with a hand pump, which provided our water in the summer.

In the winter, it would freeze up and our water had to be hauled. We all drank from an open bucket, using the same dipper, and had one bath a week whether we felt we needed it or not. This was accomplished with the aid of an old-fashioned washtub and some wood-fire heated water poured over us from pails.

Coleman lamps provided flickering light, and Mom washed our clothes in a 55-gallon barrel under which Dad would build a fire to heat the water. We had a stinky wooden outhouse way behind the cabin and near the woods. It served its purpose well, but going there was a pain, and it was tricky to use in the cold and snow and particularly at night. While other boys dreamed of being a movie star or playing pro football, I dreamed of having a toilet that flushed.

Chapter One – Hidden Secret of Cooper Creek

A couple hundred yards away from our cabin, and flowing along down a gentle slope and into the world famous Kenai River, was a little creek. It was not that big or deep, except in places where the beavers had been at work, and it was named after the town we lived in. It was Cooper's Creek and it contained a very valuable secret. I played, waded and fished for small Dolly Varden and rainbow trout in that creek many times.

It was a special place for me, but I did not know how special it really was. Dad loved to fish there, and he would sneak out early, when he said that the "big ones" were active. He had once caught an incredible 29-inch rainbow at the mouth of the creek. He reported that on at least one occasion he saw what he thought might be some small flecks of gold in the creek bed. We laughed at him about it then.

Betty Sunby was a lady in our church who always carried a little purse-string bag filled with small gold nuggets. She got along quite well and we were always curious about how she managed to support herself. Dad would visit her and discovered she was collecting small nuggets of gold from "panning" the Kenai River, right below Cooper's Creek. It did seem like a lot of trouble, however, for what she was getting. Gold prices weren't very high back then.

Well, believe me, we don't laugh now. It turns out Dad was right about those flecks—more right than we could have ever imagined. Later, a mammoth gold strike occurred right next to our cabin and on Cooper's Creek not far from where Betty Sunby used to pan. I don't recall if she was still alive when the strike happened. At any rate, untold millions have been mined from it.

I smile ruefully when I reflect on the irony of it all. We lived as paupers next to streams of gold. We were literally camped on a goldmine, yet scraping for breadcrumbs. Gold that could have been ours for the taking. It was open land and up for grabs. We could have legally staked our own claim with a simple application and a small fee at the proper state office.

Honestly, though, I think the real riches we got from our childhood were far more substantial than all the gold we missed in Cooper's Creek. That much money has a tendency to destroy. Therefore, I have no real regrets that the gold was never ours. Course, I will give you this much: I have been a little curious once or twice about what it would have been like.

I think it taught me a valuable lesson, in that we often overlook the treasures that are all around us in our continual quest to find what is on the other side of the fence. Maybe the best kept secret and greatest treasure of Cooper's Creek was really our mom. Truthfully, I cannot imagine having a more interesting life than that which I have been privileged to live and grateful to write about.

"What was that, dear? How much did you say it was going to cost to send our girls to college? Yikes! Okay, kids, grab your gold mining pans. We are going prospecting!"

Chapter Two

Feeling Big

"Boyhood Dreams"

Dad had promised to take me hunting, and I eagerly waited for that day to arrive. My wish finally came true one Wednesday night after he came home from our small church prayer meeting. He had closed early and was unusually excited. Surely, his finishing early had absolutely nothing to do with the fact that moose hunting season opened the next morning.

He said to me, "Rocky, I had a dream last night and in it I saw three moose in a meadow near some big construction pipes." He continued, "I think I know just where that is. I am sure it must be in the Kenai burn area close to Soldotna by the huge gas pipes being installed there." He paused and then said breathlessly, "I'm driving there tonight and you are going with me!"

I just stared at him. I wasn't completely on board with all this vision and dream stuff, but I didn't care. I wanted to go hunting. I mumbled, "Great, Dad, anything you say. When are we leaving?" Dad looked at me a moment, decided I was not spoofing him and said, "Seriously, Rock, we are leaving tonight. Get packed!"

Hey, you don't have to ask me twice. I was going to get a chance at my first bull moose. Dad had his dreams and I had mine.

We packed as we usually did for one of Dad's hunts: tossed everything we thought we might need in a pile in the back of the station wagon, and all six of us headed out. (It wasn't that our little toddler sister actually wanted to go, but where do you leave her? The nearest day care was 200 miles away.)

It was late and Dad drove for a couple of hours in the dark. At last, I saw a huge round shape next to the gravel road. Dad said, "There it is! Those offloaded stacked pipes were placed there for the pipeline. This must be the place."

Everyone else had already fallen fast asleep in the warm car, finding any space possible to snuggle into. Six people in a station wagon, along with lots of gear, doesn't allow for much room. It was late August and getting cold outside. At first, our parked car was warm because the heater had been going full blast, but soon it began to get very cold. We huddled and snuggled closer to preserve the precious heat.

The next thing I knew, Dad was shaking me and I came awake at once. I was too excited to stay sleepy long. He whispered to my groggy brothers and me, "We have to go before daylight and find that meadow I dreamed about. Anyone who wants to come has to get up now!"

I was already up and getting ready. My brothers groaned and mumbled something about sleeping a few minutes longer, and they passed out again almost immediately. I put on a coat and "bunny boots," grabbed my .303 British Infield military rifle, dumped a handful of bullets into my pocket and hurriedly got into step behind Dad.

The going was very tough. The Kenai burn was created by a famous massive forest fire that burned many homes and destroyed thousands of acres. We had almost been trapped in it as well, but that is another story. The blackened trees were strewn all over, lying haphazardly across each other, and thus there was almost no straight route anywhere. That, along with the muskeg (wet, boggy tundra), willow trees and fog, made walking very difficult, especially for me. I was young, holding a heavy rifle and wearing bulky boots and a backpack that contained essential gear. It didn't matter. I felt like a man. I was hunting with Dad!

This area was a haven for moose because they loved the young willows that grew after a fire and the fresh new shoots that grew in the marshy wet areas created by beaver ponds and dams. Fire leaves behind an ash that saturates the ground with a chemical compound, changing the acidity of the soil and naturally bringing out nutrients in the growth that animals love. Ingesting this growth results in the moose becoming very healthy and growing massive racks.

I had no clue where we were going, but Dad moved along with a great sense of urgency. He wanted to get to the "meadow" he had seen in his vision, and something was pulling him along. I struggled mightily to keep up and to make as little noise as possible. At last, we broke through a group of trees and came out on a little knoll. He stopped abruptly and whispered excitedly, "This is it, I know it!"

We hunkered down behind some spruce trees for cover and waited for the first light of dawn and for the fog to clear. I had no idea what he had seen or why "this was the place," but I was very glad to have a chance to rest. I was nervous and breathing heavily. Dad gave me a quick glance and put his finger across his pursed lips, indicating silence. I was afraid to breathe hard after that, but I was also very excited. I just knew something good was going to happen.

Soooo, this is hunting, I was thinking, trying to puzzle it out. Drive late into the night, sleep in a cramped cold car, get up before dawn, hike through an obstacle course and then hide behind a spruce tree. Why do hunters love this so much?

At last, the first rays of light came over the treetops and pierced some of the fog. Dad was looking intently into the "meadow." He grabbed my arm fiercely. I almost shrieked. He pointed and whispered, "There they are. I see three huge bull moose!" I was astounded. I looked and began to make out the shapes. Sure enough, there they were, and they were huge. My heart began to pound and I caught myself holding my breath. "Calm down," I whispered to myself. "Relax and breathe."

With cold, trembling fingers, I carefully loaded several shells into the rifle. Dad was smart; he never let me walk behind him with a loaded rifle. We got down and waited for a clear shot. Dad was down on his left knee and had his trusty .30-06 aimed at one of the moose. We had seen three, but now I could only see two. They were about 150 yards away. I knew Dad would aim at the biggest one, so I aimed at the next largest. I tried to hold the rifle still. Boom! Boom! Dad was firing and so was I. I thought I saw his moose go down. I continued to fire at mine, boom, boom, boom! I don't know how many times either of us actually shot, but I saw my moose go down too. I was thrilled. I had shot a big bull moose!

Then I looked again and saw that a moose was up and starting to move off. Oh, no! He was getting away. I looked at Dad for help. What he said shocked me. "Son, I am out of bullets. How many do you have left?" I checked. I had one bullet. We did not have a clear shot, so this last bullet had to count. I felt like my childhood hero, Davy Crockett, who often hunted with only one bullet. We began to rush toward the wounded moose to get close so I could end his pain. I saw the moose come to a stop and start heaving, so I was certain we would get near enough for me to finish the job.

We had only gotten about halfway when three men off to our right began yelling at us. "That is our moose! That is our moose!" What? Huh? What were they talking about? That was my moose! They came stomping up and stopped a few feet away, confronting us, standing abreast. Each one had a rifle held menacingly in front of him, and I was very sure *they* were not out of bullets.

The one in the middle had a scruffy beard and fatigue army issue pants and shirt that were both too tight, and he wore a beat-up, brown hat. He looked as if he wanted to beat us up. The one on his right had a big smirk on his face and red wavy hair and wore jeans and a dirty flannel cotton shirt. The man on his left wore a camouflage outfit, sported a thin greasy mustache and was chewing tobacco.

I had seen his type hanging around the saloons in town. He spit some tobacco juice in our direction, tapped his fingers on his gun for emphasis and said menacingly, "That there is our moose!"

I glanced at Dad and he was just as calm as a fat, grazing farm cow, although we both knew he was standing there with an empty gun. From the easy manner he held it at the ready, you wouldn't know that *he was out of bullets.* I had to admit, the man could bluff, and he was cool, but what was he going to do? He couldn't let them take that moose. My moose. I quickly looked to where I had last seen him and he was ambling off. Oh, no! Guys, figure this out quick, please. Then I began thinking. *Figure it out? Hey, wait a minute, these dudes could shoot us.* I sure didn't want my dad to get shot over a silly moose. Heck, I didn't want to get shot, either!

"Yeah," the greasy moustache continued, "that there is our moose, cuz you already got yer two. That's right; both of them went down right over there." At this, he pointed with his rifle barrel to where I had seen Dad's moose fall. I noticed Dad instinctively flinch when the man waved his gun.

Then what the guy had said sunk in. We *still* had two moose down. But didn't the one I shot get up and run? How could that be? Of course, there had originally been three moose, and in the confusion, we had shot at all of them. Two moose had stayed down. That explained this last moose.

Dad said, "Alright, fellas, we thought one of ours had gotten up, so you better hurry after the one that is getting away." Wise decision, Dad. They outnumber us and have loaded guns. Get the three of them moving *away* from us. These preachers are sharp!

We returned to where we had originally shot at the moose, and sure enough, there were two moose down. Their antlers measured 52 and 54 inches respectively. Anything over 50 inches is considered a trophy rack, and this was my first one. I was so happy. I knew I would be the envy of every kid I knew—especially my brothers.

We set about processing the moose. Dad strapped a messy pack on his back filled with a hindquarter and headed back to the car. He told me to find something to pack out too. After he left I just stood there gazing at those horns. I had gotten my first bull and he was massive! I felt like Superman. I felt big. I could now conquer the world. An adventure will do that for you.

The decision on what to pack was easy. I am sure you would concur. I grabbed those wide antlers, put them on my shoulders and headed out. They were heavy and bulky, but I was pumped. (You've probably already figured out that this was not a very smart thing to do.) It was still foggy in patches and I was in heavy terrain. It was the first day of moose season in a popular hunting location not far from a drivable road where trigger-happy hunters might be waiting in ambush, and I was carrying large moose horns around my head.

It is a wonder I was not shot, but it never even occurred to me what a dangerous thing I was doing. I was in too much of a hurry to show off those horns to my brothers. It was a rough pack, but I was filled with adrenaline, and when I burst through the last of the trees and saw our car, I was almost running. It was then I stopped dead short.

Dad had seen me, and his face told it all. He was horrified, came charging at me and yelled, "Put the horns down! Put them down!" I did so, and quickly. When he reached me, he gave me a big hug and said, "Son, don't ever carry horns on your shoulder in the wilds or you will get shot." At first, I wondered why someone would shoot me and then it registered. I blanched, very embarrassed at my stupidity, and replied meekly, "Yes, Dad."

He smiled and said, "Let's go make your brothers jealous. It will serve them right for staying in the car." Now he was talking. That's what I wanted to hear. He picked up the horns and carried them to the car for me and, boy, were my brothers green with envy. I think they are still mad at themselves over it to this day. I don't think either of them ever bagged a set of horns that large.

Well, the fun part was over and the arduous job of processing and packing began. We only had two decent backpacks, so some of us had to carry the bloody pieces in our hands. It was tough and the mosquitoes and moose flies were everywhere. I was afraid a grizzly or a wolf would come after me when they smelled the fresh blood. That gave me energy for the packs and I hurried, especially through the denser areas.

Mom told me to bring her the moose's heart, and I did, placing it on the hood of the car, causing fresh blood to run down the fender. Mom set up a propane stove next to the car and whipped out a cast iron frying pan. She sliced some onions and started preparing moose heart and fried onions, a true Alaskan delicacy.

She often did this with caribou and moose tongue as well—also Sourdough specialties. I had only walked off a few feet after delivering her request, when I saw a man in a military car drive up and stop next to her. He was a member of the territorial police. They dealt with big game violations. Mom was beautiful to me, and I had noticed that men often liked to chat with her. I paused and waited, being just close enough to catch what he might say. He looked at the moose heart on the hood and at Mom. His hat was tilted back on his head. He was acting kind of cocky and officious. "I see you got a moose."

Mom got that sarcastic look on her face again. I could see a big twinkle in her eye. Oh, I wanted to hear this, so I edged closer. She slowly moved the hand holding the knife up and brushed back some of her thick hair.

She turned and looked directly at the official, bloody knife still held high. She looked at the moose heart, then back at him and said, "No, officer, I didn't. I just cut his heart out and let him go!" The officer looked as if he had been punched. He opened his mouth to speak and then shut it quickly. Just as quickly, he stepped on the gas and scattered dirt and gravel getting out of there. Mom and I laughed our heads off.

We were happy because we had good meat for the winter. We were like the Indians and their buffalo. We actually ate every part of the moose except for the "grunt," (a low guttural sound). And this year, it was moose meat that I had helped harvest. That made it taste even better. Each time I took a bite; I would remember the hunt and feel proud. Moose tasted better than caribou, which we usually relied on. Getting two moose was divine provision. I have never admitted this to anyone, but whenever Dad tells me now that he has had a dream, I listen!

From Childish Play to Lifelong Passion

In the previous couple of chapters, I included some of the stories of my childhood in Alaska to provide some entertainment and background as to why I have grown to love the wilderness so much and to give the reader some insight into why I chose the profession of big game Alaskan guide.

I think that when I initially contemplated becoming an Alaskan big game guide, I was just trying to find a way to combine my love of Alaska and obsession with the great outdoors in a way that would be both challenging and rewarding for my family and me. My California wife was a tough sell, but eventually she graciously supported my dreams. Without her love and devotion, none of this ever would have happened.

The rewards that I have received as an Alaskan guide, though, have been far beyond what I expected. Interestingly, the greatest benefits have not been financial. I have truly been blessed beyond measure watching young people, aspiring men, established men, famous men and everything in between as they have come to grips with themselves and faced down their inner fears.

I have seen this occur in our four daughters and my wife as they dealt with the rigors of remote Alaska for months at a time. I have watched our daughters turn into confident young ladies, and I am convinced the wilderness had a big part in that. It has given them a wonderful perspective on life that is hard to duplicate.

Cooper Landing log church, hand cut, hand peeled by my brothers, me, Dad & a few church members.

Dad was a Baptist preacher, and although I squirmed a lot in my seat when he preached, there was one time he got my full attention. He was reading from the book of John, and the following verse immediately became my favorite:

"I'm going out to fish," Simon Peter told them, and they said, "We'll go with you." (John 21:3)

How about that. Simon Peter was a fishing guide. If it was good enough for him, then I am in good company.

I was still a young man when our family moved from Cooper's Landing, Alaska, on down the Seward Highway a few miles to Moose Pass. Moose Pass was several times the size of Cooper's Landing—that's right; it boasted a population of over three hundred! Our school even had three rooms. We were big time now, and of course, we continued to have some great experiences.

Later, we moved about a hundred miles north to Anchorage. I was simply awed at the size and modernization of this city, although it would likely be viewed as primitive and modest compared to most large cities stateside. It is, however, the largest in Alaska. Nearly *half of all the residents* in the state live there. That makes rural and remote Alaska incredibly less dense by comparison.

Alaska is over twice the size of Texas, larger than the 22 smallest states combined, about a fifth the size of the entire Continental United States, (Lower 48) and yet much of the state is so uninhabitable and rugged that not many people live outside of its few major cities and towns. Most of the population is concentrated in four cities and their surrounding areas, Anchorage, Fairbanks, College and Juneau, the state capital. The rest bravely exist in small, mostly isolated, rural towns and scattered, remote villages.

Only one city has over 40,000 people, and only three other cities and towns have over 10,000 people. Wyoming is the least densely populated state in the Lower 48, yet it is five times more densely populated than Alaska. The average person per square mile in Alaska is just one brave soul!

After a few years of mulling over books and confusing theories offered in higher education as to why we exist and what it all means, I returned to my roots in the Alaskan wilderness. The lessons learned there have been invaluable and greatly exceed any that I received in school. In fact, I have discovered that our created earth is an amazing manuscript, an infinite school for learning.

I believe the following experiences will intrigue and amaze you as much as living them has inspired and challenged me. I think these adventures have shown me much of the heart of a man, and what drives him.

Thus, I offer you more real adventures depicting the ongoing quest of men, boys and even a young lady taking on extreme elements in their drive to test themselves and find what lies within their souls. Several young men began their rite of passage to manhood and discovered the beat of their own heart. You may even find that yours beats a little faster too, and compels you to start your own quest . . .

Chapter 3

A Son Stands Tall, Facing Down a Charging Grizzly

"Grizzly Bear Teeth" Photo © 2009 Rocky McElveen

Chapter Three

A Son Stands Tall

"Everything I say can be fully substantiated by my opinion."

I'm a people person. I know how to get along with almost anyone, whether likable or not. My livelihood depends on it. My family relies on it. Nevertheless, there are those times when you meet someone who initially rubs you the wrong way. Sometimes you don't even know why. Maybe it is something that is triggered in your subconscious due to a trait they have, or something that brings back memories of another time and really has nothing to do with them or the present situation.

Whatever the reason, you may get to a place that you dream of strangling them and believe whole-heartedly that if the judge and jury knew this person like you did, they would give you a medal for taking them out. In your fantasy world, you know you would not just be acquitted, but applauded.

When I meet a new client, I have usually talked to them for months on the phone and listened to their heart and excitement about their upcoming trip to Alaska. I am their new best friend, and we often develop a real bond and become true friends for life. They see in me a "rock" in the middle of this unknown adventure they are undertaking.

Some grow to trust me to such a level that they begin to share other aspects of themselves, and they may even seek to apply in their own lives the knowledge I have gained from many sojourns in the wilderness. This bonding is usually cemented even deeper during their actual experiences in the wilds with me.

I can travel anywhere in America and be welcomed into countless homes. It is thrilling to listen to these men and their families and watch their sons' eyes shine brightly as the men relive their adventures with me. Just by the way they relate their stories, I can tell they have recounted them passionately and often. We frequently laugh and cry late into the night, especially when they tell me how their Alaskan journey has changed them.

Then there are others whose connection with me takes a different road, a bumpier road with odd turns, frequently bringing them and me to places of introspection, yet with amazing potential for growth. The first one that comes to mind is Kevin Shirk. We called him "Kev"—Kev from California. He had been to Alaska before, with another outfit. He was young, handsome, fit and a very successful Southern California businessman.

He also was used to being in control. He had to be. His business was cutthroat and Kev was called upon to make quick and sometimes risky decisions, often on the spot. He was good at defining how things would be. He was a man who knew what he wanted, and he was planning another trip to Alaska. He had hunted worldwide and knew the score. Ever since the birth of his son Trenton, he had dreamed about taking him to Alaska. Well, the moment Kev had longed for those many years had arrived, and Trent, whom Kev had dubbed "T", was turning 14, and would accompany him. This would be T's birthday present, a gift for both of them.

When I received the first call from Kev, we did a lot of talking and planning, but nothing developed and the trip did not occur. He called again the next year and the same thing happened. I get these types of calls often from people who want to relive their prior adventures. Who better to discuss it with than a professional guide, right?

Sometimes I feel like a doctor to whom everyone wants to relate their latest surgery or injury. Or a cop who tries to slip away from the group when the topic of a car accident or citation arises. So, when my wife Sharon got the call the following year from Kev and handed me the phone, I grimaced and said, "Here we go again—his annual call."

But this time was different. When I received the deposit for his trip, I was floored. The primary concern as we developed his trip was that he wanted to do a lot in a few days. He was planning to hunt for three different animals plus fish for several varieties of fish and salmon. I wanted to facilitate the adventure for him, but Alaska not only has a way of changing our perspectives, it really seems to delight in playing havoc with our agendas.

I feel compelled to interject a suggestion for the first-time Alaskan visitor, a bit of advice for those who want to go to Alaska and "do it all" in one short week: Don't, please. You will never stop long enough to enjoy yourself and may ruin your week trying. This is clearly not the way to visit Alaska; it is sort of like trying to withdraw money from your own checking account at the bank—while wearing a ski mask. Things will go south in a hurry!

Some clients want to fish for salmon, northern pike and Sheefish, photograph all the scenery, get a wolf, hunt ducks, shoot a caribou and a moose and then toss in a black and brown bear hunt to top it off. Yikes! Please don't use a shotgun approach when you visit Alaska. Pick one or two things you'd love to do, and really relish them.

Save up and come back. Forgo a few tanks of gasoline for that SUV, and the savings probably will pay your airfare. But, however you accomplish it, rest assured, you will never regret it. It would take many lifetimes to explore Alaska fully, yet still probably only scratch the surface. I have wandered the Alaskan wilderness for almost 50 years, and I learn something new each day in the wilds. It is truly our last fabulous frontier. I hope it stays that way.

On the surface, the main thing Kev sought sounded solid. He desired a week with his son in the mountains of Alaska, a week to bond and to heal parts of their relationship, even though overall it was a good one. Kev was sure of the formula he sought, and although I thought we were on the same page, we weren't. He wanted to be flown to a remote spot and dropped off with adequate supplies and support.

He and T' would hunt, fish and allow the wilderness to do its magic. What Kev expressly did not want was to be "trapped" at a remote lodge together with a number of other father-and-son duos. That sounded too much like a soft, comfortable camp to him, and he wanted more than that. (In fact, nothing could be further from the truth. The father-son week is the real deal, a highly sought after remote wilderness adventure and very different from a simple Boy Scout week.)

There are outdoor father and son games, guided fishing trips, hunting, wild game dinners, camping and cooking on the river and the camaraderie and competition that develops between the fathers and sons as well as between the sons with each other is quite remarkable and special. It is often a favorite week of mine, too, because it is so much fun to see sons and fathers bond and having fun in the awesome outdoors.

Kev's real plans did not fully register with me. Maybe I didn't listen closely enough to his heart. Somehow, I believed he actually desired only a couple of days in a remote drop camp, even if he thought he wanted to spend a full week there. He also wanted to fish, which is best accomplished from the river-based lodge where I have boats and gear. Men often tell me they want to be flown into the almost inaccessible wilds and left for days, and I smile inwardly. Very few really enjoy more than two or three nights in that setting, as it can get pretty lonely and hairy.

I figured Kev and T' would really be happier spending a portion of his week at my Holitna River Lodge, which is certainly remote enough. I was convinced they would thoroughly enjoy the company of other dads and their sons, sharing stories, fishing, river hunting and enjoying this beautiful setting. Most fathers and sons tell me afterwards that it is the highlight of their trip.

So, I scheduled several days for them at the lodge. Little did I know that I was inadvertently placing a full can of gasoline on a roaring fire. You see, I'd made some assumptions about Kev that were incorrect. I assumed he was like other dads who had come with similar plans and been very appreciative when I modified them. In this case, I was wrong.

I factor in many things when I make such decisions, though. I particularly like the mobility and flexibility I retain when hunters initially stay at the lodge. From there, we can fly at a moment's notice to where the target animals actually are in the field, set up camp and maximize chances for a successful hunt. This is much easier and more cost effective to accomplish than trying to relocate a drop-off camp already in place.

Caribou in particular are quite nomadic and are on the move constantly.

Thousands can be in one area one day and 30 miles away the next. I go on scouting flights to locate the various herds and often can predict where they will be in the next few days. Using this information, I position the hunters so they will have a terrific chance of harvesting a dandy trophy.

I knew that Kev wanted a caribou and a black bear for himself and a caribou for his son, so in planning his trip, I arranged it with these thoughts in mind, thinking I was doing my best to accomplish this for them. But, as the saying goes, "Even the best laid plans . . ."

To add to the brewing turmoil, and for reasons not associated with the trip or with me, Kev was angry inside and particularly mad at God and anything associated with God. Kev's mother had been killed in a car accident several years back, and a short time later Kev's childhood girlfriend had been killed. His father, a devout man of faith, was dealing with cancer and facing death. Kev felt that something was wrong somewhere with this world and that whoever was running things was making a big mess of it.

I do confess that I have been in that frame of mind a couple of times myself. Kev did not want any connection with anyone or anything that sounded the slightest bit religious. There were only two or three people he knew whose faith he genuinely respected, because it matched their lives. One of those was his father who "walked his talk," remained steadfast and never wavered in the face of tremendous tragedy and pressure. Even so, Kev and his dad had reached an uneasy truce in which discussing anything spiritual was off the table.

To Kev, "fundamental Christians" in particular were to be avoided at all costs. He had come to believe that they had hidden agendas, were judgmental and only wanted to get close to him for what he could do for them financially; thus, he distrusted them immensely. He would rather go to a bar and hang out with people who seemed "real" and were authentic, at least from his perspective. He agreed with Billy Joel's famous line, "I'd rather laugh with the sinners than die with the saints."

Kev had concluded that someone needed to take control, and the best man for the job was probably himself. He knew instinctively that the wilderness would be good for him and his son. Kev would have signed with the previous outfit he'd been with, but was fearful due to the lack of support they maintained in the field. This was critical, since his son was going to be with him. Kev had seen how fast the weather in Alaska could shift, where one minute it

is delightful and serene, but within moments can deterio-
rate so badly that those caught up in it may struggle to
survive. This reversal can be unreal. One moment you are
the happy, carefree pigeon, and in the next you are the
statue!

Kev checked around, found out about my operation
and eventually decided on a trip with me; in part because
I had a lodge that itself was remote and was a great staging area for drop-off camps. That provided an extra level of
safety and support to those brave souls wanting an unguided venture in the wilds. This seemed to be the perfect
fit for him.

After much discussion and preparation, Kev and his
son T' began to make big plans for Alaska. Thousands of
dollars were spent, new rifles and gear purchased and
many evenings wiled away chatting about their upcoming
adventure. Kev was happy. All was moving according to
script, and even the trip preparations were bringing his
son and him closer together.

This all seemed providential, because T' was going
through a particularly hard time with his mother, Kev's
ex-wife. The expedition would come at a prime time that
could be the start of healing for the whole family, or so Kev
hoped. He and T' worked out, hiked over nearby hills and
got into great shape in anticipation of the packs they knew
they would face on the slippery tundra of Alaska's mountains. T' was an all-star basketball player and was confident he could keep up with anyone when the time came.

T' could hardly sleep the night before their trip. Soon it
was time and they were off.

Almost immediately, things began to go wrong. Upon
arrival in Anchorage, they discovered that their luggage
had not made the trip with them. In fact, it had been sent
to Colorado. Happily, Kev had scheduled a two-night stay
in Anchorage before his flight to the Holitna Lodge. They
spent two days at a second-rate hotel with only the clothes
they wore and no toiletries, and missing over five thousand dollars worth of gear.

This was just swell. But in spite of it all, Kev made do and he and T' enjoyed exploring Anchorage. They especially got a kick out of taking a stroll at midnight without a flashlight and visiting the Lake Spenard/Lake Hood seaplane airport, the largest and most active of its kind in the world.

Although they wouldn't know this was an issue until later, the next problem arose when Kev attempted to buy hunting and fishing licenses and game tags for T'. The vendor selling tags and licenses in Anchorage told Kev that T' did not need any because he was a minor. Not only was this incorrect, but anyone caught shooting game without proper credentials and tags is immediately arrested and their guns and equipment are confiscated. It is no joke. Alaska treats big game violations more seriously than almost any other felony. Shooting a brown or grizzly bear without a tag is at the top of the no-no list.

To their immense relief, late the second day all their luggage arrived intact, and none too soon. They were due shortly at Merrill Field, a small airfield in Anchorage that handles light aircraft. They met several other father-son combos there, and all were taken in a 16-seater twin-prop plane out to a small native village, Red Devil, which is a pick-up point for the lodge. It was then that Kev learned he was the "rookie," because the others had all been to my outfit before. They came up to him and were very friendly, often commenting, "We've heard a lot about you."

Kev thought it was nice that all the dads were so conversational, but he was a little put off that they seemed to know him. What was up with that? He is a private man, and after all, he wasn't going to be with this group very long, right? He didn't want to be. It wasn't that he disliked them or would not have enjoyed their company in another setting. He had come to Alaska for different reasons. He wanted to be alone in the wilds with his son.

Their flight took them over mountain passes and glaciers, and T' and Kev both were awestruck. The views were truly magnificent and Kev was delighted to share this with

T', who had never been in a plane so small or seen mountains of ice this large. Kev relaxed. Finally, the expedition was starting to get off on the right foot.

However, on their approach to the narrow gravel runway in Red Devil, the young pilot came in too hot and offline. The plane hit loose gravel, skipped sideways, yawing and pitching, and every man and boy in the plane went white-knuckled, tightly gripping their seat or whatever else they could grab. Kev heard a few quick prayers being sent heavenward. He, too, had the Lord's Prayer racing through his mind. The landing especially freaked him out because his son was on board.

Somehow, the pilot managed to get the fishtailing plane under control and stopped it safely at the very far edge of the runway. When it came to rest, Kev heard an audible collective sigh of relief from all aboard. Kev glanced at the pilot and was surprised to see that he was grinning broadly and appeared to be having a ball. These Alaskans were a unique breed. What a strange way to get a rush.

Upon deplaning after that heart-stopping landing, Kev and most of the men needed to make a quick trip to the bushes next to the airstrip. Once the foliage was duly watered, they returned and noticed an outgoing group of men along the runway who were waiting to leave.

These men had numerous caribou  horns, bear hides and wax boxes full of fillet salmon set out, stacked up and ready to be taken to Anchorage. Seeing all those antlers and salmon got Kev, T' and the other new arrivals all excited and filled with anticipation. Kev grinned at the wide-eyed stare and gleam he saw in his son's eyes.

I assigned two pilots and planes to fly to Red Devil and begin the process of ferrying this group to the Holitna Lodge. Once they were at the lodge, Sharon, and our four girls greeted them warmly, making them feel right at home. And we all began calling Trent by his nickname, T'. By the time I got the entire group transferred, it was too late to consider moving Kev and T' to the field, even if I had planned to do so.

I also wanted to check out one of the plane engines to make sure it was safe to fly, because my pilot had reported some irregularities. Safety is always my number one concern. I had not planned to transfer anyone from the lodge to the field this early in the week, however. I had a hidden secret. I knew of a large herd of caribou that was moving in, but they were still many miles away so it would not do much good to send anyone out yet.

Kev, though, fully expected to be moved immediately to a remote drop-camp site right after he arrived at the lodge. He became upset when this did not occur. And he was very surprised to be met by our four daughters and Sharon. Our daughters are all beautiful, a real handful, lots of help and loads of fun, and a couple were near T's age.

T' was delighted about this new wrinkle, but Kev was not happy about it at all. The girls were tickled because T' is a nice looking young man and an all-around great kid. Kev did not have anything against the ladies per se, but he did not want any interference between himself and T'. Staying at the Holitna Lodge with attractive ladies would be a major distraction.

I realized immediately that Kev was unhappy and set up a nice late evening guided fishing trip for him and his son. I sent a great guide, Josh, with them, and they had a terrific time and landed a number of nice salmon and northern pike. T', I could tell, was having a blast and he and Josh connected right away. They returned late and I gave Kev one of the best cabins, the only one at that time that actually had a generator, so I knew they would be comfortable.

The next morning, Kev again expected to be rushed out to a remote hunting site. He became frustrated when he realized this was not to be. He complained to John, the cook and head guide, "This is not what I paid thousands for! Do you even realize how much money I have spent? This is not what I was promised."

T' was supportive of his dad, but he was having a great time with Josh, our girls and other sons his age, fishing, boating, watching the wildlife and relishing the beautiful remote setting. That boy was just too handsome, though. I made a mental note to keep a sharp eye on my daughters.

The second day arrived and Kev determined he would be flown out that day. He figured he had lost two hunting days and if I wasn't going to get him out in the field pronto, then he was already considering going back to Anchorage and finding another operator who would.

The plane engine passed the safety check-up, and I had a good idea where the caribou I had seen were headed. I instructed the pilots to begin flying out the hunters and setting up the various drop-off sites, positioning them in the areas I felt would be the most promising. I had planned to have Kev flown to what I thought would be the best spot of any in the group. I scheduled him to fly in last because this is usually the favorite slot of the hunters.

I wanted Kev and T' dropped off last because of the "fair chase" law, which requires that hunters cannot fly and shoot the same day—a great law that gives the wild game fair warning that you are there and allows them a little time to disappear.

(Hmm, that might be a good rule for our daughters on their dates: No kissing allowed on the first night—or how about never!)

Anyway, hunters arriving later in the evening don't have as long to wait before they can hunt. Just before Kev and T' were supposed to leave, I asked to see their licenses and tags. To my dismay, I learned that T' did not have his. Oh, great!

I was stuck. I had no choice. To rectify the situation, I asked one of the best pilots, Jacob, to fly T' to Sleetmute, a sleepy remote village about 40 river miles away (a river mile is about 3 to 4 times greater than point-to-point). It was becoming very late and they would have to wake up the local resident who owned the general store there. He obliged, but was understandably grumpy about being disturbed. What a pain this was! Understand that the cost is $300 to $500 an hour, plus pilot wages, to fly the planes. You can imagine just how expensive that tag and license turned out to be.

Kev and T' were firstly flown via a six-seater 206 to a handpicked field staging location with a decently worn down flat dirt landing area. From there they were flown in a two-seater lightweight Cub to the drop-off camp. T' loved all these flights and could not believe how small this last bush plane was. T' said later, "I thought the 16-seater that

brought us to Red Devil was small; next I flew in the six-seater and that was really small; and then I flew in the two-seater bush plane, and that thing is tiny!"

He was right. There is only room for the pilot and one passenger, who sits on a very low seat directly behind him, knees bunched up, and from that position is able to touch both sides of the plane with his elbows. T' stashed a small bag, his rifle and some gear in the tail of the plane. T's eyes got very wide when he saw how low they flew, but it was awesome for him to see moose, bear and thousands of caribou as they passed only a few hundred feet over their heads.

T' stiffened when they descended to land in the gathering darkness. Where was the landing field? This was almost too thrilling, landing on the side of a mountain in fading light directly on untested tundra, hoping to not hit a boulder, bush or solid clump and flip over. Man! These guys were nuts. What a ride.

T' was flown in first, and Kev remembers watching him fly off in that tiny plane and being separated from him for the first time on the trip. That was a jolt. He started thinking, *Gosh; if he gets in a crash, my ex-wife will have me in court the rest of my life.* Kev was glad when he safely rejoined T' not long after, but he was not happy about the lateness of the hour.

They could not hunt until the next day, further trying Kev's patience; he had seen thousands of caribou during his flight. Later, he and T' watched several herds come within a couple hundred yards of the camp, their huge horns outlined against the skyline. Kev sat there dismayed. He could have already been here hunting those trophy racks, racks that might be gone in the morning. Of course, to Kev's credit, he didn't know that it would have been difficult for me to pinpoint their path that far in advance, and as it was, I had been right on the money.

I flew in afterward to join them and brought in one of the new guides, Billy, to hunt with Kev. Billy was 53, but in very good shape. He had guided elsewhere, but this was his first time in Alaska and, curiously, Kev was the first client I had ever given him. I chose Billy because of his obvious maturity and mild disposition, in hopes he would gel with Kev.

We all got to bed quickly and had visions of all those caribou we had seen running around in our dreams. Naturally, the next day when we awoke, eager to hunt, the caribou with the big racks were nowhere close by. You see, our education system in Alaska is not that bad after all, and 'bou are obviously apt pupils. They know the score too. They know "what time it is!"

As we continued to search, scouting the area from a hillside, we spotted two huge bull caribou over 500 yards away. Something spooked them and Kev watched helplessly as they ran toward another hunting camp of guys from our group. A bow hunter from that camp also saw the bulls.

As Kev sat on the hilltop observing the show, it was indeed fun watching the bow hunter stalk and harvest the smaller of the two bulls with an arrow. It was not fun knowing that if the bulls had continued on their original path, Kev or T' could have shot them before they were spooked. That smaller bull turned out to be the largest taken by anyone the entire week. The larger one definitely would have been a trophy animal.

The four of us continued hiking and hunting and at one point were positioned on the side of a mountain, lying on our sides to stay out of the skyline, eating blueberries, taking in the spectacular scenery and using binoculars to look for game (referred to as "glassing"). I saw an absolute monster brown bear and her enormous three-year-old cub a couple of miles off prowling near some caribou. I pointed this out to the group, and we all watched them.

T' said, "That grizzly is huge. She looks like a minivan even from this far away." Kev said, "That is the biggest bear I have ever seen—even bigger than the one in the glass case at Anchorage Airport."

I was thinking how cool this must surely be for Kev and his son and what a different world for them. Cell phones are useless, there's nothing modern and the food is gathered from the land, not a grocery store. Yes, this is a land and a place where control is given back to nature and if not given, taken. I can't script what happens here and neither can anyone else, however powerful they may be elsewhere. That is part of the magic and tantalizing allure of this frontier.

We hunted the rest of that day and the following morning and saw many caribou but no bulls large enough to warrant shooting. I had smiled when we first got up and Kev and T' were physically very sore, especially since they had bragged about what great shape they were in. T' said, "I was in great basketball shape, but this is totally different." Billy, however, was motoring up and down the mountains like a goat; soon Kev and T' nicknamed him "Billy Goat."

They could not believe that a 53-year-old man could hike the pants off them. I saw that they were developing a real bond with Billy, so I left them later that morning to go check on the other hunters. I could tell that Kev was having a wonderful time trekking and sharing the wilderness with his son, but I could also sense he was unhappy that they had not bagged any animals. I sent up a silent prayer that they would meet with success, and set about tending to the other guests, who conversely were all harvesting some beautiful 'bous. Dang! That doubtless would be salt rubbed on an open wound once Kev found out.

Kev and T' continued to hunt with Billy the rest of that day and saw the huge brown bears again, but still had not seen any big bull caribou. Kev was getting more discouraged. They were coming up on the fifth day and he knew he was running out of time. Billy was a calming influence, though, and told them to be patient. Morning again dawned cold and clear and, boy, did they wake up stiff. Two days hiking in rough terrain for miles and their legs were screaming for mercy. Billy prepared some lukewarm coffee and they contemplated the coming day's hunt.

They had noticed that most of the caribou they saw were traveling along a ridge on the far side of the same valley in which they had seen the bears. They decided to cross the valley and intervening hills to investigate. During this hike, they had many obstacles to overcome, hills to climb, creeks to cross, and then (naturally) it began to rain. They got so tired on one hill that they simply lay down and soon were fast asleep, ignoring the pelting rain falling all over them.

T' said later, "It was kind of odd. When you are on an Alaskan mountain in the middle of nowhere, your issues back home become small and are forgotten. In fact, as I lay there getting soaked, I began to reflect on the problems Dad had been going through and the tough things I was dealing with, and the strangest thing happened. It was almost as if this wilderness rain was washing my troubles out of me. I was thinking, *If I can survive here; I can deal with anything.*"

After a good rest, they got up and continued to the ridge and peered over. Sure enough, there were no caribou to be found. Not one critter. It is said that the "ghost of the north" is the wolf, but Kev was beginning to feel that bull caribou must be a kindred spirit. They returned to camp and naturally, just as they arrived, there those beauties were! Over 300 caribou were moving quickly on another ravine about a mile away, with cover in between.

Billy said, "We have to hurry and try to get in front of them." He set out at a run. Kev and T' needed no second invitation and scrambled to catch up with their guide, who was racing tirelessly ahead. Keeping up with Billy was proving very hard to do, and rapidly traversing a mile in heavy brush, grass and slippery tundra was immensely tiring.

Kev said later, "I thought I was going to die! I kept telling myself, Keep moving, keep moving."

At one point, they came parallel to the route of the caribou, which were still out of sight in an adjacent draw, but they had to scale almost straight down a steep ravine. Billy was fearlessly flying down the hill and yelling, "We gotta outrun them!" Kev and T' looked at each other and just shook their heads. They couldn't let an old man show them up. Down the hill they sped, chasing after Billy Goat.

Caribou tend to take the same routes over these hills and ridges year after year, but determining the dates and times is a real puzzle. It is amazing how narrow these trails near the ridgelines are, and it is imperative to keep tightly to the path because a misstep can be deadly.

Moving quickly but carefully, Kev and his son managed to keep close to Billy. At last, Billy stopped and got down into a crawl, inching up the final ridge overlooking the caribou. He held his thumb up and motioned for them to get down. He pointed to where the herd was located.

All right, they had done it. They were in front of the herd and very excited as they slowly crawled to the edge and peeked over at the oncoming herd. More and more of them came into view. More and more cows! Not a single decent bull in the entire crowd. What a bummer. What's going on? Was this ladies' week only? Was some type of bad vibe at work?

Kev stared at the herd, trying vainly to conjure up some big horns somewhere. No bulls showed up, though. It was getting late so they headed back to camp. They crossed back over the ravine and, picking a slightly different route, wound up fording a creek heavily surrounded by alders. They began to walk parallel to the alders through an open meadow. Kev was discouraged and deep in thought.

Billy was in the lead by several steps, followed by Kev with T' a few feet to the rear. Suddenly to their left they heard a loud crashing noise. They all froze in their tracks. Straight out of the alders and between Kev and T' raced a cow caribou. She saw them and stopped stock still, breathing heavily, feet splayed wide. The initial crashing sounds and startling appearance of this animal jump-started Kev's heart and shocked him speechless.

She was barely 20 feet away and obviously scared, evidenced by her sudden peeing and wide-eyed stare. After a couple of moments and sensing no danger, Kev relaxed and continued to watch the caribou in amusement, wondering what she would do. Then, from behind him, he heard T' quietly repeating slowly but urgently, spitting each word out with emphasis, "Dad, Dad, bear! Dad, Dad, bear!"

Billy was electrified by the sharp voice too, and he and Kev quickly looked at T' and then to where he was pointing. They gasped at what they saw. About 100 yards off was a huge eight-foot, 700-pound boar grizzly. Then they realized that the bear was looking at the terrified caribou and the caribou was staring right back. The lady was truly in a tight spot. Three men on one side with loaded guns and a hungry grizzly on the other with ferocious teeth.

Abruptly, as if she had been stung by a scorpion, the caribou leaped high and fled across the meadow past the three men and the bear, probably setting a personal best in her quest for speed. She was gone in a twinkling, but the bear was not gone and now he began eyeing them, probably accusingly. He was decidedly unhappy about losing dinner.

They watched, fascinated, as the grizzly started getting agitated, pacing back and forth quickly, then standing up and sniffing the air and beginning to make low growling sounds. Billy said, "I think that bear is going to charge us!" They huddled up, talking fast, keeping a wary eye on the bear.

Kev said, "There is nowhere for us to run or hide. If we go into the alders, we are doomed. That is his backyard." Kev then asked T', "Are you good? Are you okay? Is your gun loaded?" T' replied, "I'm okay; don't worry about me. My gun is ready to fire!"

Kev said, "I don't want to shoot him if I can help it, and so far he hasn't done anything to us. He is a gorgeous bear, and none of us has a grizzly bear tag anyway." Billy said, "I don't want anyone to get arrested for shooting a brown bear without a tag. It is hard to prove self-defense in Alaska." Well said, Billy. It just might be harder than getting a kid to clean their room.

The growling of the bear was becoming more audible and he was starting to snap his jaws, a sure sign he was agitated and getting ready to act. Then Kev had some scary thoughts. Was this was the same three-year-old cub they had seen with the monster sow several times in the last week? It sure looked like it. If so, where was the sow? If she was nearby, would she feel they were a threat to her cub? Was she behind them or in the adjacent alders? Had she been the reason the cow caribou had been flushed out of the trees? Were she and the cub working as a team?

Kev had shot a 300-pound black bear on another hunting trip. It had taken 11 bullets to subdue it. This brown bear was more than twice the size of that black one. And this bear, if he charged, would be very difficult to hit on the run, especially anywhere vital. Bears can move at amazing speeds for short distances.

Kev, Billy and T' had only loaded three or four shells in their rifles. This meant they collectively had available 10 or 11 rounds at most, and if the bear got close, it would be difficult to maneuver a long rifle effectively. Kev decided to use his .45 auto with its 13 rounds and close quarter advantages. He laid down his rifle and grabbed his handgun.

Billy was hanging tough. He had been in pressure situations before, but this was the first time he had faced a mad Alaskan grizzly. He tried to think. What would Rocky do? If this bear was killed, he knew there would be a nasty investigation and possible criminal charges, so he had to stop the bear somehow without killing it.

He knew in his gut the bear was getting ready to charge. The bear had that same aura of a mad bull in a ring ready to rush the red cape of the matador. Billy knew that he, Kev or T' would likely be killed, and painfully. What a legacy! You or your first client killed, mauled to death by a wild beast. Why was he thinking that? Focus! What were his options?

T' was awestruck. He had never seen such raw power this close up. He gripped his gun tightly. He had done well at the target shooting range but had never shot at any type of wild animal in his life, not even a squirrel or rabbit. Would his or his dad's life depend on those untested skills against a charging brown bear? He did not want to die today. He glanced at his dad standing next to him. Dad seemed confident, and T' drew strength from that. They would team up and stop this bear if he came at them.

They chatted quickly and all agreed they could not run or hide, so knew they would have to face this bear head-on. The bear began walking closer, stalking to one side, then the other, frequently standing up and staring hard at them, sniffing the air constantly and shaking his massive head. The three of them had shifted and were standing side by side watching this spectacle, waiting for the explosion each believed would come. They kept whispering to each other, "You good? I'm good. Be ready. Okay, everybody all right? We'll make it. Hang tight!"

This went on for about a minute when unexpectedly the bear dropped to all fours, reared back and lunged forward. This was it! Here he comes! They braced themselves collectively, fear racing through their hearts. Billy whispered, "Wait, wait, don't shoot yet, wait."

Kev rarely got scared, but this was different. He was used to standing toe-to-toe with anything that came along. But now, he was terrified for his son. When the bear had gotten about 30 yards closer, he skidded to a stop, stood up, front paws swinging in the air, and let out an ear-splitting, ferocious roar, a primitive guttural sound that chilled each person to the bone. Wow, this was one ticked-off bear. T' could not believe how fast the bear had gone those initial 30 yards.

The three had instinctively bunched closer together, taking strength one from another. Kev pushed T' down next to him. "Get on one knee and get a bead on that bear. If you have to shoot, make each shot count."

Kev glanced at Billy and said, "How close does he have to get before we should shoot? How close before it is really self-defense?" Billy looked and saw a little spruce tree about 30 yards in front of them, between them and the bear. He said, "If he charges past that little tree, open fire."

Kev asked his son, "T', you got that?" T' nodded vigorously and immediately searched for reference points to establish the spot he would need to start shooting. Kev stood beside T' and held his .45 firmly in his right hand, pointed squarely at the unpredictable bear. T' was down on one knee and locked in. He flipped his hat bill around backwards so he could see his gun sights better.

The young man was in a zone, calm and thinking clearly. This sudden calmness surprised and thrilled him. He knew his dad had his back. He knew that his dad would not let him down. He mentally rehearsed where he would aim and the steps to re-chamber another round.

Billy positioned himself behind T' and aimed his rifle over T's shoulder. They were each in place and ready, the three pressed together as one. Everyone fell silent, waiting for the decisive moment. This whole scene had taken about two minutes to unfold. Enough time for their hearts to start pumping out of control, enough time to come face to face with their own masculinity and courage and enough time to have the sure knowledge that this experience would forever change them.

Each had his own specific focus. Billy was looking at the bear and at the spruce tree, trying desperately to find a solution other than shooting this magnificent animal before it reached that tree, the point of no return. Kev was looking at the bear and the tree and then anxiously glancing down at his son. What had he done? *Brought his son up here to die or be chewed to pieces?* His ex-wife would kill him. Who cared about that now? This bear might do the job for her!

T' was his eldest son, and his kids were his life. He glanced at T' and grinned at the cap turned backwards, sensing the meaning and knowing his son was focused. He saw that T''s rifle was rock-steady and Kev felt pride surge through him, giving him confidence. He would not; he *could not* let T' down. He would die first if he had to, to protect his son.

Kev realized, with surprise, he was praying silently. It was the first time he had prayed like that in a long time. Meanwhile, T' was feeling good. His body was steady and it puzzled him. His focus was strictly on the bear. He knew he was in good company and did not have to worry about Dad. This was his moment, his time to be there for his father. The bear was in his crosshairs and he was not going to miss if that bear passed that tree.

The bear was getting more and more agitated, standing up and tossing his head, baring his teeth and growling, his cheeks loosely flapping and saliva drooling down his chin. The hair was standing up on the hump of his back, and he continued to wave and cross his arms in a swimming motion in front of him, the sun glinting off his long, black claws.

He would sniff and sway from side to side, all the while staring at the huddled group now only 60 yards away. His ears looked ridiculously small in contrast to his mammoth head. Abruptly he paused, still standing upright but stock still, glaring hard and long at the bunched threesome. Had he made up his mind? The answer came swiftly. He opened his mouth wide, displayed massive teeth, shook his body violently and then with a mighty, thunderous roar dropped down on all fours and charged straight for Billy, Kev and T'!

Someone yelled, "Oh, God! Here he comes!" Each stared intently, watching this powerful, majestic beast flying at them with incredible speed, eyes boring into them. It was a moment that was forever imprinted in their minds, the awesome force of nature fully unleashed. Billy was horrified, knowing shots would soon ring out—death was in the air.

Kev was fixated on this surreal scene, his prayers spitting rapidly from his mouth, sounding like pistons at full throttle, the lessons from his own dad surging from his soul and bolstering him in this time of need.

T' felt an intense sensation growing inside of him and knew he was gearing up for battle. His body was becoming electrified. The grizzly had just about reached the tree and wasn't slowing down. The time for chat had passed. The time for waiting had ended. It was time for action.

At that same moment, Billy felt an uncontrollable urge to meet force with force. The raw manhood within him had taken over all logical thought. From a primitive place in his brain, he was compelled to rise. He reacted instantly and launched his body forward at the charging bear and directly in front of Kev and T'!

He thrust his arms upward, disdaining aiming his gun, and heard himself answering the bear with his own roar, the strange raw sound coming from deep within his stomach, as if he were mimicking and mocking the on-coming beast.

Billy began waving his arms wildly, shaking his head and rocking his body side to side. Billy's actions took Kev completely by surprise. Kev was astonished. At first, he couldn't perceive what was happening, but Billy's gyra-tions triggered a primal response in him as well, and in a split second, he found himself alongside Billy, growling at the top of his voice and swinging his arms. One part of his mind was screeching, *What are you doing? Are you a total idiot?* The other part was snarling, *Show that bear who is boss,* Kev. *Choke him out with your bare hands!*

T' was thoroughly shocked and disoriented, his gun having been knocked sideways when his dad charged for-ward. It was a wonder he didn't misfire. What was going on? Were these guys nuts? Then he, too, felt a fierce fire within him envelope his entire chest, then burn across his body, and he immediately reacted. He surged violently forward rising to his full height. He split the space be-tween Kev and Billy and began hollering insanely.

Strangely, at this moment, T' felt stronger and more like a he-man than he had ever felt in his life. The three of them stood there as one unit, T' in front slightly, Kev to his right and Billy to his left, shouting, whooping and swinging their arms, guns and bodies crazily. Meanwhile, the huge, raging, charging grizzly bear had just sailed right past the spruce tree.

I don't know if a bear can truly register surprise on its face but if so, this bear did. Within moments after passing the spruce, he shot his front paws out jointly and firmly into the tundra, and managed to slide to a screeching halt 20 yards in front of the three men. In the process, his mouth dropped wide open, his tongue swung to the side and he jerked his head backwards as if avoiding a blow.

His growling slowly became a mild rumble and he just remained there a moment, motionless in a semi-sitting position due to his big rear-end sliding forward under him and almost into his front legs as he skidded to a stop. He gaped and stared at them, appearing completely baffled.

They began yelling even louder, "Go away, bear! Run! Git! Go! Go!" They continued to make as big a silhouette as possible, frantically moving their arms. The bear just gawked at them, perplexed. After a few moments, the bear stood up on his hind legs and began audibly sniffing the air. Then he went back down to all fours, swung around, walked a few feet to the side and then stood up tall and sniffed again.

Billy said, "I think he's going to leave. I think he's going." Kev all the while was proudly noticing that his own male cub, his son, T', was standing just as tall confronting that bear, never showing fear, not even deigning to point his gun at it anymore. It was a moment that bonded the three of them in a magical way, permanently.

The bear ultimately started ambling off, but was not in any hurry. This was just too much to take in. He would pause, turn around and stare at the three, sniff, then move further away. He did this a number of times before he disappeared into the alders. I would like to have heard his conversation with his big old mama sow that night in their den:

"Hey, Mom, you won't believe this, but I was chasing a caribou and the strangest thing happened. A weird looking animal spooked it and that made me mad. I charged that animal figuring to make it my meal instead, when out of the blue it rose up and came at me. It had three heads, six

arms and six legs, and howled like a pack of wolves. It was a monster!"

I am sure Mama looked at Junior and replied, "Son, have you been at those spoiled blueberries over on hooch ridge again? You know your dad would get crazy whenever he partied over there."

It was an intense adventure. When the bear was completely gone, Kev, Billy and T' felt their bodies sag and relax. They sent up a prayer of thanks not only for their survival but also for the bear. They couldn't stop thinking about it, but for the moment, there was nothing to say. They high-tailed it back to the tent mostly in total reflective silence, each soaking it all in, each realizing that one or more of them had probably just escaped death.

Once they arrived at camp, though, they discussed it at length, still amazed at the turn of events and their collective response to the bear. Billy cooked up a simple Top Ramen meal that tasted like a five-star gourmet offering.

Before going to bed, Billy looked squarely at T' and said, "You stood tall, son, you stood your ground." T' grinned broadly and Kev had to look away to hide his pride and emotion. His cub had begun his own rite of passage in a huge way.

He said to Billy, "We will be in debt to you till we die. That split-second decision saved our lives and the bear." That night they laughed, giggled and cried reliving the event, each telling their version, glad to be alive. It was the type of night that is impossible to plan or easily duplicate. Kev felt a lot of his pent-up anger and frustration begin to melt.

At the end of the day, their bodies crashed and they curled up tightly in their sleeping bags, yet slept fitfully, their minds still energized from the experience. The next morning Billy had to leave to help me. I was starting to evacuate all the camps. I scheduled Kev's the last to leave because I wanted to give him as much hunting time as I could.

I asked John, the lead cook and an excellent guide, to walk from his camp to Kev's camp to replace Billy, as I didn't have an available plane in the area to move John there by air. John walked probably six or seven miles through very rough terrain, and forded one large creek and numerous ravines and hills to get there. He never complained. Upon arrival, he began hunting with Kev and T', scouring the surrounding hills and valleys looking for a decent sized bull caribou. Again, nothing.

It was just one of those things that happens and can't be explained. The other camps did great. It was like being on a fishing boat where everyone is using the same bait and same technique, and all are slamming the fish except one person who never gets a hook-up.

Kev was bummed about the fact they had been shut out. Because of this, Kev did not want to be flown out. He got on the radio and started telling the pilot, "Don't pick me up. I am not coming out." He wanted more time to hunt. I reorganized the evacuation and agreed to let them stay one more night. I certainly wanted Kev and T' to have a successful hunt too.

The next morning Kev got up early and snuck out of the tent. He looked up on the hillside and was delighted to see two nice bull caribou outlined on the ridge exactly 205 yards away. He quietly re-entered the tent and whispered, "T', get out here! There's caribou. Get out here!"

Kev was particularly excited for T'. This is what Kev had dreamed of for years. This is why he had come to Alaska, to see his son shoot a nice animal. This is what all the target practice had been for.

T' was ready. He got his gun, and using the tent for cover, got on one knee. Kev kept whispering to him, "Wait till he turns. Be ready. You got 'em, T'." Kev had his rifle trained on the caribou, too, in case T' missed. The caribou turned broadside and Kev said, "Take him, T'."

T' was fully focused, strap locked on his arm, and aimed carefully. Bang! The caribou went straight down, shot clean through the heart! What a great shot, especially for a very first try. Kev and John ran up the hill to the 'bou. What was T' doing? He was pacing off the yardage natu-  rally. It was 205 yards on the nose. What a gift and special moment for father and son.

I was very happy about T' getting the caribou. I went in and helped break down their camp. Kev was really glad for T', but still did not want to leave. He felt he had at least one more day left, and he had not gotten any of the animals he sought.

When I had him flown back to the Holitna, he was disappointed. I understood his frustration about coming up empty, but I was happy that at least he had experienced the most wonderful present he could possibly have had in sharing the incredible events with his son.

At the Holitna, John went to Kev's cabin to talk to him and sat on the bunk bed. Kev's long week of frustrations had boiled over and he said, "This is the worst outfit I have ever been with, and the worst guiding experience of my life."

He glared at John and continued, "They have robbed me of my money. This is not what I paid for! I want to get out of here right now. If this is the way it is going to be, I will go to Anchorage and get a reporter and let all of Alaska know what a rip-off this is!" He added angrily, "After that, I will go to the Better Business Bureau and file a complaint." Kev's disappointments had at last come to a head.

At that juncture, John stood up, and of all things, inadvertently bumped into Kev, who stiffened but John held his ground. He said, "Come on, Kev," and slapped Kev across the shoulder with a folded up newspaper. T' was in the room and his eyes flew wide open. He had seen his dad upset before. He fully expected blows. Not that his dad looked for fights, necessarily, but because he was not one to back down.

The two men stood facing each other. Something in John's calm manner told Kev no insult was intended. He relaxed and the two men talked for a while. Kev sensed that John understood where he was coming from. Besides, he did not have an issue with John. He knew the problem concerned the misunderstanding between him and me. In the end he said, "I need to talk to Rocky."

John informed me that Kev was waiting to meet with me outside his cabin. I sighed and went to see him. He started right in on me. We stood there jawing at each other and then I made a decision. I said, "Kev, I just wanted this week to be the best experience for you and your boy. Apparently, it has not been that for you. Tell you what. I will personally guide you and T' up the Ho-Ho on a river hunt tomorrow. This will be a special trip. I don't do this for many people, and there won't be any extra charges."

We continued to talk, and during that conversation, something began to happen in both Kev and me. He cannot explain it fully, nor can I, but he began to see that I was not just another in-your-pocket church guy out to take his money and force him into a specific agenda. He discovered that I cared about him and his son. I discovered that I had misjudged Kev.

Taking him on the trip to the Ho-Ho was a real sacrifice for me, though. It was the last day Sharon would be at the lodge, and I desperately wanted to be with her. We had things to do, and frankly, I would miss her.

I woke up with a rather sour disposition about leaving Sharon, but I put on my happy face and said to T' and Kev, "Let's go. Those bears and wolves are waiting for us."

I also took Josh, because he and T' had hit it off so well. The Ho-Ho is the sister river to the Holitna River and they join up a few miles below the lodge.

I took the fastest boat and away we went. I knew where there was an alpha-male wolf with at least six in his harem. I also had seen some black bear near that area. I hoped that Kev would get a chance for at least one of these animals. As we progressed up this winding, treacherous river, we began to dialogue. I told him in depth about the wildlife and some history of this part of the woods. This was my backyard and my home. I tried to make him feel connected to it.

I resented leaving Sharon, however, and this exhibited itself in my boating. I began to race the boat upstream and fly around tight curves and over shallows. Once, I had to swerve violently at the last second to miss a floating log that could have capsized us. In so doing, I nearly hit an overhanging "sweeper" branch that missed T' by inches. Instead of getting angry, everyone seemed to revel in this daredevil ride. It served as a type of release. The close brush with disaster seemed to accelerate the bonding process for all of us.

After coming close to the log, I gathered my senses, slowed a little and chided myself for being stupid. We went about 50 miles upriver. I am an excellent "river runner" and can maneuver through areas most others can't, allowing the clients more opportunity for game others can't get to. I kept at it hard because I was seriously trying to put Kev on a black bear, the primary animal he sought, and also take him and his son to places few have ever been.

On the way, we stopped often and foraged ashore looking for game. It was great getting to know T', and the better I got to know him, the more I was impressed with this young man. Kev had done a great job raising his son, and their relationship was special. That increased Kev's stature immensely in my eyes.

Well, you probably know what happened. Kev was snakebite this week. We didn't see any of the game he wanted to shoot, and returned empty handed. I could tell Kev wasn't thrilled about being shut out, but at least some bridges were being mended. He knew I had tried. After he and T' flew out the next morning, though, I never expected to hear from them again.

Kev said he began to reflect about the whole trip on the long flight home. Then, over the course of many months, he started to realize that his incredible adventures in Alaska were far greater than what he had anticipated or imagined. What had really happened to him was that a father and son had experienced something that few in the world ever would. Someone greater than he or I had been at work and designed the perfect trip. Someone had given him a special gift.

Reliving those events with his son in discussions with other people, something in him changed. People could see it and often commented on it. Kev says, "My son and I were forever changed." Kev also met the love of his life a few years ago and attributes his change as part of the reason their marriage is getting even stronger. He is a different man from the one who went to Alaska. He is a better man and father.

Kev knew he had to return to Alaska, and this time he wanted to take his dad, his son and some of his close friends. Whom did he call? He called me. When asked why, Kev says, "I just knew, I knew." He adds, "And when I called Rocky, he welcomed me like the prodigal son."

I think Kev expected me to be angry, and I will admit we had parted on uneasy terms, but I had the utmost respect for Kev. I was actually glad to hear from him. When I picked up the phone I said, "Oh, my gosh, Kev, how are you? It is so good to hear from you." I meant it. I was happy he called.

Kev then said, "Rocky, after that trip something has happened in my life, and I want to ask for your forgiveness." I was very touched by this and I replied, "No, Kev, it is I who needs to ask for yours. I have been resentful toward you and that is not right."

Amazing. What an interesting guy Kev turned out to be, and what a wonderful conversation we had. We did not know it then, but we had bonded in the wilderness and those bonds run deep. This was just a part of our ensuing friendship and the continuing growth for both of us.

T' had drawn strength from his father while facing the grizzly. Kev had released some of his rage at life while confronting the raging bear. Do you suppose the Creator designed Alaska and its wilderness in such an amazing fashion that an adventure there can transform  lives and affect us in ways few other situations can? I know I do.

In many travels across America, I often pass through Southern California. And guess what? I almost always stop in to see my friend Kev. We often enjoy a nice round of golf or a backyard barbeque, but the fun really begins when we growl at each other in unison and try to imitate those famous snarls that foiled the grizzly.

Chapter Four

Wilder to the Rescue

"The *Plane* Truth"

Have you ever had a guilt-laden conversation, or something similar, with your spouse, kid, parent or maybe an authority figure? You are trying to convince them to believe you, especially when the facts seem to state otherwise?

"No, no! For real, this time it actually wasn't my fault! You gotta believe me."

"Sure, Mr. 'Fast Talker,' you and that golden tongue of yours have wheedled your way out of hot spots before, but this time I am not buying it!"

"Please, now, come on, trust me. This situation is so different. I am telling the honest truth, and I can prove it. I know it looks bad, but if you will just hear me out and give me only two short minutes, then I can explain . . . everything. Please?"

"Ay yay yay! Why do I fall for this? Okay, you have 60 seconds and this better be good."

I was in more than a run-of-the-mill hot spot. I was in very deep trouble. I could see no way out. I faced the loss of my life or the loss of my freedom, along with the ruination of my career. How had this happened? My mind swept back to the start of the trip . . .

Several daredevil pilot friends and I had planned a trip to the Nushagak Hills with three quite powerful and rich executives from the automobile business. Maybe that should have been a tip-off, maybe not. I must add though that it is truly sad the reputation that some occupations have—only because a mere 99 percent of them give the rest a bad name!

Well, they wanted to fly in and hunt where the big trophy caribou were and, if successful, then possibly spend a couple of days hunting for bear. Now, the trophy animals didn't get that way by being stupid. They find the toughest terrain they can to forage and hide from predators. I knew of such a place in the Nushagak Hills, about 80 miles out from the lodge. The landing areas would be difficult, but worth the risk to hunt this area and give the clients a chance at some of these beauties.

It was late in the fall and the snow cover was already inching its way down the higher mountains, blanketing Alaska with its beautiful white winter coat. We call this "termination dust." The leaves were gone, the warmth of the summer was a distant memory and the interminable winter was fast approaching—the ageless cycle.

Snow was beginning to fall on our gravel airstrip creating slippery take-offs and landings during the early mornings and late evenings. The days were just barely warm enough to melt overnight frost and snow. The stinging cold of the long Alaskan winter was beginning to settle in and lock the land in its icy grip.

The men who come to Alaska to face the wilderness during these conditions are a special breed. Some have no *clue* what they are getting into or doing—much like the guy who said, "Hey, who invented the *brush* they put next to the toilet? That thing *hurts*!"

This is even truer of seniors, reminiscent of the following story someone emailed me:

A senior citizen was driving down the freeway and his car phone rang. Answering, he heard his wife's voice urgently warning him, "Herman, I just heard on the news that there's a car going the wrong way on I-10. Please be careful."

"It's not just one car," snapped Herman. "It's hundreds of them!"

This particular outing occurred earlier in my career. I was working with three pilots, each of whom lived near my first lodge and staged from the same gravel airstrip that I did. One of them had a relationship with an Alaskan wild-life trooper who frequently stopped in for a visit. He was a big man and, unlike most of the larger men I've met, was not soft spoken. Let's just call him Hooper—Hooper the Trooper.

He had a commanding presence and, like the Alaskan sled dog, was diligent and thorough at his job. He made all of the guides nervous, and some of them should have been.

He knew about my operation and, for reasons I have never understood, detested me. Just before we flew out on this trip Hooper came up to me, pointed his finger at my chest and said, "Everybody I have ever known who went by the name of Rocky I have put in jail, and you will be no exception. I am going to put you behind bars!"

I blanched at this bold assertion, looked him square in the face and said, "Now, why in the world would you want to do that?" He curled his lip and replied venomously, "I have heard all about you, Rocky! I am going to pull your ticket!"

I didn't know exactly what Hooper had heard, but I honestly wasn't concerned. I had always been very careful to follow regulations, and the wilderness was my home. I cared for it and wanted it preserved as much or more than any state agency did, and besides, my livelihood depended on my integrity.

I did know, though, that among guides there was an uneasy truce, much like beauty contestants at a pageant. They would be sweet and syrupy to your face and cut your throat behind your back. This was especially true if you were successful. Someone always wanted to bring you down and might drop a dime with some juicy but false info at any time. I knew of two in particular who were bad-mouthing me, and I wondered privately if they had gotten to Hooper.

I just grinned broadly at Hooper and said, "Say, if you want me to get you some delicious caribou sausage, just let me know. I think I could spare some tasty portions and still make the 143-pound meat weight requirement."

The 143 pounds I was referring to was the amount of dressed meat you had to make when you brought in a caribou. This was not always easy because sometimes animals were shot in meaty locations that rendered that part unusable, and oftentimes bear and other predators would get to the animal before you could fly it out of the woods. Hunters without a bear tag are expressly not allowed to protect their downed game with deadly force.

I was excellent at processing game in the field, however, and never once failed to make the proper amount of weight. Besides, I think wild game is nutritious and delicious, so it baffled me that anyone would knowingly let any of it go to waste.

Hooper had waited on a number of previous flights as they arrived from the field and had weighed the meat himself. I just shook my head whenever I saw him patiently waiting for a return flight. I knew of guides who weren't as scrupulous as I was, and I was puzzled as to why this trooper didn't seem to go after *them* with the same vigor. In over 22 years as a big game guide, I had never received one valid violation, and with all the various agencies and regulations involved, it is hard not to make at least some mistakes, no matter how careful you are.

I have always enjoyed a very good relationship with the Alaska Fish and Game and other State personnel. I even store equipment for them over the winter in one of my cabins. A number have stayed at the lodge, freely landed on my airstrip and use it on occasions for various field exercises. The lodge is always open to them and I have nothing to hide. Several of my family and relatives are currently in law enforcement, or have retired from that career, so I appreciate wholeheartedly the job the troopers do and get a kick out of the crazy stories they tell me when they stay with me.

I guess I am saying that almost all of the state troopers with whom I had dealt were squared away folks. They quickly ascertained that I respected the laws of the land and moved on to those guides who didn't. But not Hooper. He turned red in the face, puffed himself up and said, "I have been told to watch out for you, and you better curb that mouth, buddy! I am going to own you."

Well, that rankled some because in my heart, no one owns me. Course, where my wife is concerned, I might make some concessions. At any rate, I bit down hard and managed another big smile. I looked at him and said as sweetly as I could, "Sir, you probably couldn't scrounge up a proper down payment for me. I hear that the price on my head is up to 50 dollars these days!"

He stared at me a moment, likely trying to decide if I was being funny or a smart-aleck, promptly gave up, turned on his heel and stomped off. As I have said, I respect the law deeply, but that profession (as in any other) occasionally has someone with a personal grudge who gets too emotionally involved, and thus their thinking gets clouded. I hoped such was not the case here, but I continued with my preparations with an uneasy feeling.

We had two PA-18 Cub bush planes and a Cessna 180 at our disposal. The pilots found a decent spot on the hilly slopes to land the planes and began ferrying in the men and supplies.

We quickly set up the tents and I prepared some hot grub for our guests. One of the pilots stayed in a tent next to mine. Let's just call him Neon, because he was a bright spot on this adventure. We chatted a bit before turning in. He said to me, "Rocky, with your gift of gab you could charm a mad, wet wolverine, so with these clients I want you to do all the talking and I will do all the walking."

Neon is a good-looking guy, in great shape and a terrific pilot. He had turned more than a few ladies' heads in his time. I grinned at this and said, "Neon, you know what we say about you, don't you?" He glanced at me a little startled, and then shook his head. "We say that Neon is made of twisted steel, religious zeal and sex appeal!" Neon burst out laughing at this, but I could tell by the faint smile that lingered on his face that he was secretly pleased.

Neon and I then cut out a niche in the alders in which to place the one Cub that we kept at the location. I used a new, special *Cabela's* tool with a nifty saw in it to cut the alders. Neon was amazed at how effective this little gadget was. Soon we had a nice safe place in which to back the plane. We stabilized it even more by tying it to the alders around it.

I had seen many *Cheechakos* (Alaskan rookies) and various other newbies to the bush whom we generally referred to as gringos. They were unfamiliar with the unpredictability of our Alaskan weather and the deadly rapidity with which it can change. Unwittingly, they might not adequately secure their planes in the field. After an unexpected storm, if they weren't on top of things, they may discover to their dismay that their neat little bush plane has been upended, blown off the ridge, whisked down the mountainside, or tossed into inaccessible terrain and damaged beyond easy repair.

There are many stories of pilots who have had to tie down their planes as securely as possible and then sit in their plane in storms, thus providing valuable extra weight. They face their fragile craft into the wind, and may have to keep the prop turning just to hold the plane at a standstill. This is an expensive and tiring way to keep their plane aground and safe, but sometimes it is the best option if there is no other way to secure it sufficiently against strong winds.

The bush plane is the lifeline of those hardy souls who make the wild their permanent or even temporary home. They guard them for the same reasons and with the same tenacity of a prospector providing for his donkey or the passion of an eagle protecting her young.

Soon, we all turned in and awaited the chilly dawn to begin our hunt. As I lay in a cozy sleeping bag, I unaccountably began to smell the faint aroma of pot.

Chapter Four – Wilder to the Rescue

The smell seemed to grow stronger, startling me to attention. I sat upright in the sleeping bag and blinked. I was wide awake and could definitely smell the pungent odor of weed. I carefully and quietly exited the tent and investigated. Sure enough, the executives in the other tent were having a good ole time smoking hashish.

I blanched almost as white as the snow. Using drugs was something I neither did nor condoned, so this was not good news. However, neither being nor wanting to act like a cop, I figured it was none of my business. Hooper would skin them alive if he showed up. Yeah! Where was he when real crime was afoot? I eased back into the sleeping bag and prayed that the executives would use up the last of their supply that night.

I drifted off into troubled sleep and was actually glad for once when dawn broke. It was foggy and chilly outside, but as is my custom, I preceded the others getting up and fixed some grub and hot coffee. The executives were surprisingly alert considering their previous night's activities, and so I relaxed a bit. I advised them to be careful with the metal utensils because the noise created by clanging them together carried far in the cold mountain air and was not a natural sound in the outdoors. Any unnatural sound in the wild will alert the prey you seek. Therefore, we chatted quietly, the breath from our mouths forming a smoky mist in the morning light, a sort of miniature replication of the splotches of fog that floated aimlessly among the ridges around us.

I think that this time in a hunt or adventure is one of the most telling and exciting. I see great eagerness and excitement in the faces of the clients getting ready for their first day in the wild, mainly because the time for talk has ended and the real deal is about to begin. I see the true person begin to emerge. Some have talked big for months and bragged about their prowess and abilities. Some have asked me tons of questions prior, and have brought everything but the kitchen sink to make sure they are ready for everything and anything that might occur.

I look into their eyes and watch them as they get their gear and stuff together. Reluctance here, fidgeting there, anxious glances and excessive trips to relieve themselves are common. This and other behaviors may innocently reveal a sense of just who they are. Even though I have done this a long time, I still get amused and sometimes even surprised at how the clients respond in the field.

The three executives were nervous but itching to go. Let's just call them Pops, Smith and Jones. Pops was a bit older than his cohorts, but seemed in decent shape. Jones and Neon set off toward some promising ridges where we had spotted "'bou" on the previous day, and Pops and I set off in another direction. Smith decided to hunt on his own for a while. I walked slowly at first to allow Pops to keep up, but he did fine so I was able to increase the pace.

Caribou are very nomadic. They do like specific routes; however knowing when they will be on one is pure speculation. It is usually best to sneak up on ridges, sit for a while and glass (scan with binoculars) the area. Once they are located, it is imperative to stay downwind as much as possible and move quietly but quickly to a point that will intercept them, as they are always traveling at a good clip, even when eating.

I always wonder if "Rudolph" gets up in the morning and says to "Dancer," "Honey, let's go for a walk," and they walk all day, resting in the afternoon. Day after day, it is the same story. That is the life of the caribou. If any guide tells you he knows where the caribou are going to be the following week, month or year, be very suspect. The caribou don't even know where they are going to be.

Pops and I were sitting on a ridge, both to catch our breath and to glass the area, when, from the direction where Neon had gone, we heard a bunch of shots. Realizing the shots probably had scared any decent animals out of the immediate vicinity for the time being, we headed back to camp, taking our time. Once we arrived, we were greeted by an excited Jones who told us of his successful harvest of a very nice bull caribou. He proudly showed us the rack he had packed out and it was indeed splendid. I looked over at Smith, who had beat feet back to the camp, as well, and detected both happiness and jealousy. I just smiled to myself. These guys probably competed in business too.

The sight of the horns energized Pops, and we set off again at a good walk. We were sneaking along a ridge when I saw something I haven't seen before. It was a completely albino caribou. Pops and I both were awestruck. I have seen an albino wolf, two albino moose (extremely rare), a completely white grizzly bear (spotted 1,000 miles south of where polar bear would range) and this albino caribou. Now, this caribou was not just an albino with a solid white coat; it had a massive rack. I suspected it might even be a world record for its category, especially since it was such a rare animal.

Through binoculars, I could see it was simply gorgeous as well as incongruous, with its pink nose looking so out of place on a wild animal in the Alaskan wilderness. The tune "Rudolf the Red-Nosed Reindeer" began to sift through my mind. We were too far away for a good shot, so we hustled down the ridge to get closer. We had gotten to within about 225 yards when I sensed we needed to stop. The animal was getting restless and we had little groundcover to use.

I don't usually get overly excited when guiding clients, but I was pumped just seeing this animal and even more at the prospect of getting it. What a wonderful full mount it would make. The display would amaze and enthrall many future generations of all ages, especially kids. I watched anxiously as Pops caught his breath and got down into a kneeling position. He secured his weapon on some shooting sticks (braces on which to place your gun to assist in aiming and holding your gun steady) and sighted in.

I began to fret that Pops was taking too long. Then the weirdest thing occurred. A small patch of fog simply enveloped the albino caribou. What amazing cover that fog provided. It was not thick, but it blended in perfectly with the 'bou. I watched, fascinated, as the caribou just disappeared, as if by magic. The fog functioned like a giant eraser gently rubbing out the caribou from our view. I knew the caribou had not moved, but had simply become invisible right before our eyes.

I was struck with an ironic thought: *When I grew old and enveloped by the fog of years, would I be erased and not leave a trail for family or friends? Would I just vanish?*

Pops was using a powerful scope on his rifle and was trying desperately to spot the caribou, but to no avail. The wispy fog may as well have been a solid block wall. The albino caribou became an unseen spirit. In fact, the whole episode felt very spiritual.

I recalled stories of the Indians treating albino buffalo as spirits and attributing to them special powers. The Eskimo and other natives of the north did the same with the albino animals they encountered. I had never given these interpretations much credence before, but now at least I could understand why they had become lore.

I was determined to see this caribou ghost. I stared fixedly at the spot where I had seen him last and impatiently waited for the fog to drift past. It did, taking only moments, but all I could see was empty space where the caribou had been standing. It was as if the fog had not only hidden the caribou, but somehow had drawn it up into invisible air. Neither Pops nor I could believe it. We rushed to the spot where we had last seen "Casper," but Casper had vanished. We just stood there, looking in all directions, watching and hoping the caribou would somehow reappear.

I am sure it did, but not in front of us. It probably has reappeared all over those hills. I even lie awake sometimes and wonder if it truly was a spirit. Nah, of course not, that caribou was real. However, it was still an eerie experience. I named it the "Ghost of Nushagak Hills."

I want to make a quick comment here that might surprise you: I am never very sad when an animal gets the best of the clients or me. That was certainly true in this case. A part of me was happy that this caribou would live to haunt others, and I would not be surprised if that rascal haunted those hills for a long time. He certainly has roamed my thoughts once or twice.

Pops was understandably disappointed and so was I, but we both felt blessed to be privy to such an unusual occurrence. We trudged back to camp and he decided to call it a day.

I fixed lunch for all and then Smith and I set off in search of a nice caribou for him. I watched Smith as he hunted in earnest. He was very intent and determined as he and I searched for a nice animal. He kept talking about the "huge horns" of the caribou that Jones had gotten.

We took our time and as is my pattern, I stopped frequently to look for game. As I sat on one ridgeline and took in the beauty of the hills, noticing the snowline gradually inching down the mountainsides, I was infused with a sense of peace and a feeling of restoration. This invigorating environment was amazing, and I loved to ponder its power as I relaxed and breathed in the pure mountain air. I think it was beginning to have an effect on Smith too. He seemed to calm visibly as we continued to hunt.

It is during those times that profound thoughts often invade my mind. *Okay, so what is the speed of dark? How much deeper would the ocean be without sponges? What would happen to me if I got scared half to death—twice?* Seriously, though, your mind does seem to shift to real priorities in life and deep reflection. It can be very grounding.

Our calm didn't last long, however. We spotted a very nice caribou on a parallel ridge and it was in an ideal location for a stalk. Smith followed directions to the letter, and we were able to get in perfect position to take this 'bou. Smith made a terrific shot and cleanly bagged this beauty on his first try. I was happy for him but became perplexed when Smith started running pell-mell at the downed animal. I hustled to keep up, but Smith was flying toward the 'bou and increasing the distance between us. I saw no need to waste energy, which I would sorely need for the pack, so I slowed and took my time.

Upon arrival at the animal, Smith began shouting back at me. He was so excited that I couldn't make out his words at first. Was he okay? I rushed forward to hear what he was saying, and soon I began to get bits and pieces. "Bigger . . . ownsey!" Huh? "Is it wider . . . Tell me, Rocky!" What was he saying? Then the words became more distinct. Smith was urgently yelling "Is it bigger than Jones's? Tell me, Rock! Is it bigger? Are they bigger, wider? Are my horns bigger?" He repeated the last question just as I came alongside the animal. I could have interjected a smart retort, but actually, I was too amused to do anything but grin at him.

Smith stood there, legs braced apart, leaning on his rifle, breathing hard and staring fixedly at me, obviously awaiting confirmation that his animal and rack were superior to the one Jones had gotten. I struggled not to laugh aloud at this boyish reaction, but eventually I got my emotions under control. I calmly looked at him and said, "This is a marvelous animal, Smith. It is a gift for us to be here, to enjoy this moment in the Alaskan wilderness and look forward to the memories the success of this hunt will bring. Does it really matter if it is bigger than Jones's?"

He stood still for a moment, quietly digesting this information. He looked at the animal and then slowly scanned the skyline and pristine hills around us. I saw understanding creep into his facial features and watched him purse his lips as the truth sank in. He then turned back toward me, tilted his head to one side and replied, "Wow, that is so true, Rocky. What a gift this is."

Before I could respond, however, he straightened up and continued in a gleeful voice, "I still think it is bigger than Jones's, though!" We both laughed. I will admit that I clenched my teeth hard and just barely managed not to say something stupid to him about trying to "keep up with the Joneses."

It is truly moments such as these that reveal much. Maybe it wasn't true of Smith, but I often reflect on a comment I heard somewhere: "I guess you could say *deep down* he was superficial."

The location of Smith's caribou was quite a ways from our primary camp, but Neon and I previously had scouted the area and found another ridge where he could land his plane, and I was delighted, because it was closer to where Smith and I were at that time. I had asked Neon if he was sure he could safely land on the new ridge. He said, "Rocky, it will be a piece of cake. Don't worry, it'll be no problem."

I was happy about that now. This alternate landing area would save me a lot of hard packing over tough terrain, because I would only have to take the 'bou to that site to be flown out and not to the main camp, which was quite a ways. I processed it, bagged and tagged it, packed it to this secondary landing ridge and then got ready to go back to the camp. "Bagging and tagging" refers to putting the meat into special game bags to keep the flies out and tagging it with the specific animal tags each hunter has to obtain from a licensed agency prior to their hunt. Smith pleaded with me, however, to let him bring the horns to the main camp. I grinned and obliged, seeing how eager he was to compare his rack with the others.

(There are 27 steps in determining if your caribou rack is a trophy. I won't bother with each step, but here is a general idea of what a top rack requires: The first and most important determination is whether the horns have mass and symmetry. The mass should be at the top portion of the main beams. The bez points extend out from this main beam over the eyes. The shovels protrude from the mid-skull between the eyes; a double shovel occurs in about one out of every 5000 caribou bulls and is highly desirable. If the points' "tips of the tines" match on the double shovel, the bez points and the main beams, then perfect symmetry has been obtained. If the points are unequal, there are deductions in scoring. The "U-shaped" horns containing both mass and symmetry are the formula for a Boone and Crockett trophy. I have been blessed to have a number of record trophies.) *There will be a test later.*

We got back to the camp and Smith immediately set his horns next to those of Jones. It was very interesting. Those horns were about as equal as two horns could be. One had better features in one area and the other in another. I would have been hard pressed to score either one as better. That, of course, led to a lot of good-natured jousting between the two men about which one was best. I thought that was a fortuitous way to leave this dispute, and it would allow for a lot of enjoyable wrangling in the future betwixt them.

I am happy to report that the next day Pops harvested a dandy animal, as well. This occurred close to the alternate landing site, so I packed the meat there and placed it next to the meat Smith had gotten the day before. Pops wanted his horns at the camp, as well, even though they weren't quite as big, so we wound up with three sets of racks at the *primary* camp along with the first caribou, and two more caribou at the *secondary* site. All were ready to be flown out.

It had been a successful and fun trip and I was ready to leave. Everyone else was ready too, except for Pops. He wanted to stay another day or two and hunt for a bear, so we agreed that I would stay with him for that purpose.

Meanwhile, the pilots back at the lodge learned via radio that a terrible storm was brewing. They decided to fly in to get us off the mountain. Neon had already gotten his Cub out of the alders and readied it for the first load. One of the pilots coming in was Dave Wilder. He had a couple of years on me but was simply a great guy and an excellent pilot. He had modified his plane tires to accommodate the snow. Wilder was the kind of man you would want for a grandpa. The last pilot to come in and assist was Jude. He was a savvy businessman who squeezed a lot of revenue out of his planes. He was also tight with Hooper.

Jude and Wilder arrived at the camp while I was out hunting with Pops for that bear he wanted. I was not there to supervise the removal of the animals, horns, men and equipment. Since the pilots were anxious to get as much stuff as possible, as quickly as possible, they just grabbed everything they could and went "wheels up."

I don't know if Neon told them about the caribou on the alternate site or if they just figured they would get those later, but the result was that everything was taken from the primary camp, except for a tent. The two caribou at the secondary site were left behind. This information may sound irrelevant now, but it was to become vitally important to my integrity and career.

Pops, the last hunter left, and I were still hunting and trekking over hills, oblivious to the danger. I saw no warning signs of the storm. In fact, it was rather warm. This false sense of safety is reminiscent of a cat that is getting ready to pounce and becomes deathly still, fooling her prey into thinking all is well. The Alaskan "tigress" was ready to leap.

To make matters worse, we spotted a black bear—four ridges and several miles away. We began a long stalk. I started sweating, so I decided to remove my camouflage jacket and leave it along the route we were taking, marking the location carefully in my mind. I placed it on some bushes in *plain sight* in a clearing I knew we would come back through on our return.

Well, Pops did get that bear he desired and we both were delighted. As I was skinning it, Pops asked me to open up the stomach area and reveal what the bear had been eating. In so doing, I reached in with my hand and pulled out a fistful of what appeared to be a big ball of twine. Then I realized the twine was moving in my fingers. I was horrified to discover that it was a round mass of live worms. I reached in again and began pulling on what appeared to be a long, flat length of soft string. I kept pulling and pulling, stretching it out. About 12 to 15 feet later, I was amazed to see that I had removed tapeworms or round worms that were entwined in the intestines of the bear. This bear was saturated by all kinds of worms. Ugh!

I guess many animals (especially the meat-eating variety) have worms and parasites. However, this particular bear was really infested. At that moment, I completely lost my appetite for bear meat. I know that the natives still relish it as "Alaskan pork." It can be tasty, although it is a bit greasy, but it will usually taste like the particular food currently being ingested by the bear. Bear fishing season produces the worst flavor. I suggest strongly that if you eat any type of bear meat, you cook it at 350 degrees for an hour per pound. As for me, I made a deal with all bears right then. I silently pledged, "If you don't eat me, then I won't eat you!"

We had climbed high to hunt this bear, and I looked at the terrain that I needed to traverse to get back down to camp. I came up with what I thought was a good plan. I took the packing supplies and the bear hide and I rolled them up into a neat round ball. I then pushed the ball over the slope and let it roll down the mountain along the path we would have to take. It rolled almost a half mile and I felt smug about not having to carry it, at least for that part of the trip.

My smugness evaporated quickly when I arrived back at the clearing where I'd left the camouflage jacket. I learned immediately that camouflage is excellent at what it is designed to do. I can return to the site of a downed animal, camp, a hidden watering hole or almost any specific area unerringly. I was positive I was in the right clearing, yet I could not see the jacket anywhere. I looked and looked, and never found it. It was a tough lesson learned, and I will tell you that it is probably not a good idea to leave camouflage items in an area where the foliage is similar to the camouflage pattern. You might regret it. I know I did. That stuff works! I just didn't expect it to work on me, although many camouflage items belonging to guests (camo knives, binoculars, gloves, books, wives) have been placed nearby and have *disappeared*. I have always wanted to paint one of my bush planes a camo color—but if it went down, who would find me?

When we got back to the camp, Neon had already returned to fly out Pops, his gear and bear hide. He was in a rush to get him loaded and take off while he could. The storm had hit swiftly and with a passion, and I could tell by the big, moist snowflakes floating down that it would stick and settle in for the winter. Life was about to get tough in the wilderness, especially in the Nushagak Hills.

I knew I would be facing this storm alone after Pops left. Only one passenger can be flown at a time, and the guide is always the last one transported. I was beginning to wonder if any of the pilots would be able to return for me anytime soon if the weather stayed like this. I started feeling like a captain facing the prospect of going down with their ship.

As we were frantically loading up Pops, the bear hide and his equipment, the wind began howling. Neon yelled over the noise and told me that back at the lodge, Hooper had met the returning planes. Hooper was jumping for joy that two sets of horns had arrived without the corresponding caribou meat accompanying them. Those caribou, of course, were on the alternate ridge. None of the pilots had landed there.

Horns are not supposed to be flown out without, or prior to, the animal to which they belong. Hooper now had three sets of horns and only one caribou to match. He was already in the process of swearing out a warrant for my arrest for "wanton waste," citing game left in the field. One of the pilots had told Hooper that he had flown over the area where I had left the other two caribou, and that it was "inaccessible" by plane.

I was astounded. I told Neon that I would go and pack the remaining caribou meat on the other ridge to this campsite so there would be no question that they could be flown out. Neon shrugged it off and said, "Don't do that. You will need to stay out of the weather. I can easily land over there and get the caribou. I don't know what is going on, but I'll be back soon to get them. Be ready when I return, because I may not have much time if this storm gets any worse and settles in."

He quickly flew off into the snowy, gloomy sky and disappeared out of sight. I bet Pops was gripping tightly to whatever he could grab. The plane was skidding, bumping and sliding sideways during that takeoff. The storm was getting worse and I knew that neither Neon nor the other pilots would be back anytime soon.

The information I had received made me rather gloomy. Then I realized something as I stood there in the gathering darkness, being pelted by the increasingly heavy snowfall. I was alone in the mountains, without my warm camouflage jacket, with 80 miles of impassable land between the nearest dwelling and me, and an Alaskan blizzard was bearing down hard. Things were getting very serious, and it had happened in the blink of an eye.

I was hungry and exhausted. Knowing that any return flight for me would not be possible until the next morning and only if the storm abated, I made sure the tent was adequately tied down, reinforcing the stakes by slamming them as far as I could into the freezing turf. Afterwards, I put on the warmest and driest clothes I had left.

I am sure every guide has some interesting food combinations that, for some reason, taste delicious in the field and, conversely, rarely are eaten at home. Most involve various items mixed with Top Ramen, if water can be heated sufficiently, but there are many other eyebrow-raising mixtures too. One of my all-time favorites is banana bread and Spam. Now that is real grub. I prepared several sandwiches of this delicacy, warmed some coffee and enjoyed every morsel. Yum! My hunger satisfied, I crawled into my sleeping bag and fell into a deep sleep, oblivious to the intense storm raging outside.

Isn't it strange and ironic how the mighty, crashing waves of the sea or heavy pelting rain on your roof or howling wind will lull you into a deep, peaceful sleep?

Chapter Four – Wilder to the Rescue

I awoke many hours later, my watch indicating it was about 9 a.m. Without the watch, I would have had no clue what time it was because the snow was still falling heavily, blocking the sun. The entire area was blanketed in white, creating the illusion of timelessness. At first, I panicked because I was afraid that I might have missed any planes trying to find me, but I figured it was unlikely anyone would have tried to come for me while the snowstorm and wind were still so strong.

I knew, though, that if somehow anyone could find me, and land, they would not be able to wait more than a minute or two. The tent I was using was my favorite and the most expensive one I had. I made the decision to strike it and gather everything up into a neat bundle. I was praying one of the pilots would find me before nightfall and I wanted to be ready. I hoped fervently that I would not regret this decision.

I looked around at my temporary home and wondered if it would become a permanent one. Everything was an uneven blanket of white. I was on the side of a rugged mountain and perched on a high ridge that usually afforded a great view. However, with the falling snow the visibility was only a couple hundred feet at best. I watched as the snowflakes were being blown sideways, swirling and unerringly finding the cracks in my clothing. I yearned for the warm camouflage jacket I had lost. It was freezing and the wind chill factor was magnified because of the high ridge and nearby canyons creating their own huge gusts of wind, thus making a miserable existence even worse. I felt my body losing heat.

There were some alders in the canyon behind me and I knew that I could go carefully navigate on the slippery terrain and crawl into those and that they might provide a little more protection, but I would be even more invisible in there than I was out here in the open. I might fall asleep, possibly for good and never hear or see any planes searching for me. No one would be able to find me in there and I couldn't risk that. It was also the home of any hungry grizzlies that had not gone into hibernation yet.

This place was surreal. Before the storm, it had looked like many mountainsides in Alaska, majestic, untouched and formidable, but with proper equipment and care, not life threatening. Today it felt like I was in a far away fantasyland, remote and disconnected from the real world. It seemed as if I was on another planet, a planet with no life except me.

It proved to be a very long, cold, snowy, windy day. In order to combat the blustery chilling wind and damp snow, I crawled into the sleeping bag and rolled the tarp of the *Cabela's* tent around it, then lay curled up, waiting for rescue. Occasionally I could hear the whine of the engine of a small plane flying excruciatingly close by, and obviously searching the hills for me, circling repeatedly. It was maddening. I would jump up and wave anything I had with color in it to attract attention. I even tried to set a fire, but it would not stay lit due to the wet snow. I knew it could not be seen from the air anyway. I was beginning to feel helpless.

I tried to mark out the runway so it would be visible from the sky, and tried to stamp it down in the ever-deepening snow, but it was useless. The falling snow became so thick that there was no real visibility, and I knew that even the best pilots wouldn't find me unless they somehow got to within 100 feet. That low altitude would be suicidal for them.

Finding my exact location was asking the impossible in a time in which GPS was not commonplace and most pilots used Loran coordinates and/or flew by sight. The old maritime use of Loran coordinates was not exact, and although pilots could reliably return to a general area, this method was not optimal for locating a specific spot or hill. That left visual demarcations as the standard method of operation.

This meant they marked locations by certain landmarks. Those landmarks changed drastically and looked quite different when covered in white. Rocks, trees, canyons, hills, creeks and other markers just blended in with the other terrain when blanketed by snow, and this was made even more difficult when visibility was practically zero. Bottom line, I knew I was in trouble. Some of the most skilled pilots in Alaska flew for me, and they could not find me in this storm. Moreover, the storm was showing no signs of slowing down.

I was getting cold and I wrapped the canvas tent around me more tightly to keep from freezing. I was beginning to lose the feeling in my feet, and I knew all too well that when your extremities start to numb, it is the beginning of the slow process of your body shutting down and freezing. It was too late and dark to try to set up the tent and likely would be too difficult in the snow to accomplish that task anyway. I had stubbornly made my decision to save the costly tent. I hoped that choice would not cost me my life.

I remember seeing a roadway sign in a southern state where there were many accidents because of speeding, and it had read, "Saved a minute, lost a wife." If I froze to death in this storm, would my legacy be, "Saved a tent, lost his life?"

I began sleeping in short spells, then waking up in a panic thinking I might have missed an incoming plane. Then, seeing that it was still dark, I would realize I had not missed anything. I would shift my body, pull the tent tarp closer, wiggle around in the sleeping bag to try to warm up and then drift back into a troubled sleep. The hours dragged by and I felt my body getting colder and colder. I began to lose the sense of time and when I looked at my watch, I had trouble comprehending what the numbers meant. With the constant white sky, I couldn't tell whether it was AM or PM.

I recalled talking to a man who had been in jail for a long time. He told me that he was put into solitary confinement and that he was deep inside of the prison. He could not see outside. The small light in the roof of his cell was always on, and he lost touch with all sense of time and days. It was very disconcerting to him. It was as if one of the foundations of life had been removed, creating disconnection with reality. He felt as if he were drifting and lost. He told me that the saying "He knows what time it is" came from prison. A prisoner who knew what time it was; was "in the know." I was painfully beginning to understand what he had meant.

Thankfully, I awoke and could discern that it was daylight. I was dismayed to see that it was still snowing. I knew I needed to get up and try to get my blood circulating through my body to create more warmth. My body was stiff and it was difficult getting to my feet. I began running in place, my legs feeling brittle and my whole body succumbing to an overall sense of weakness. Eventually my body began to respond and some life began to creep back into my arms and legs. This was the third day in the mountains alone, and each hour dragged by ever more slowly. I did not know if I would live to see a fourth.

I became very tired while running in place. I lay back down, curled up in the sleeping bag within the canvas of the tent and stared at the falling snow, trying to focus, forcing myself to think. My hopes were falling along with the snow. I strained to consider what the possible options might be. I had sufficient food to last a few days, and considering the snow, ample water was available.

What I didn't have was dry and warm enough clothing or a good heating source, because the Coleman stove was low on fuel and I wanted to save the rest of that as a last resort to keep from completely freezing. The wind and falling snow prevented me from starting a good fire that would stay lit, and dry wood was unavailable anyway. The snow on the ground was too deep to allow me to put the tent back up with any success, and wrapping it around me was probably just as effective anyway. I wondered if I should at least try to do something.

If I tried to walk out, there was no place close enough that would offer more hope, and the pilots looking for me would have no way of knowing where I went. I would be unable to carry enough food and gear to last long in this blizzard. The land was impassible in many places, with the alders, canyons and creeks, so even if I knew of a place to go, I would not be able to get there.

I was 80 air miles from the lodge, which I would be unable to locate if walking, and from every angle I could figure, I had no option but to stay put and pray for a miracle. If the storm eased even a little, I was hopeful one of the pilots might be able to rescue me, but in this snow, I was concerned that they would be unable to land. At least they might be able to drop me more survival gear or heating fuel and dry clothing. In addition, if they could get a good visual they might be able to guide a helicopter in to lift me out. I didn't know what might be possible in this weather, but I knew the situation was desperate.

I began to reflect on some of the times I had faced death. I had been told that freezing to death was not a bad way to go. Apparently, your body gets so cold you just fall asleep and never wake up.

Dying that way might not be so horrible. The thought reminded me of what a friend told me once: "I want to die in my sleep like my grandfather, not screaming in terror like the passengers in his car."

Dying actually was not the thing I dreaded most. It was the process leading up to it I feared. I hated feeling so helpless. I hated being completely out of control. Survival was no longer up to me. The forces of nature would be the deciding factor.

That was very hard to come to grips with. I would rather deal with something I could fight or confront, something on which I could focus and vent my frustrations. A mad grizzly or a cold river or a critical wound was something I could fix or challenge and maybe overcome or make a clever decision and escape. However, this was bigger than that and relentless. I could not thwart the snow or stop the wind. I could not conquer the elements or the distance I would need to travel to safety. I was completely at the mercy of the Alaskan wilderness, and that was extremely unsettling to my confidence as a man, as a guide and as someone who always believed he could survive anything.

Morbid thoughts began to infiltrate my mind. How would they get me out if I died? I remembered telling a man hunting with me, who thought he was going to die in the wild, that if he didn't get to the top of the hill where the plane could land, then I would have to quarter him in order to pack him up there to be flown out. He looked at me in shock, but he quit complaining and made it to the ridge.

That is what we do with the animals. They have to be cut into smaller pieces to be transported. I wondered how many portions it would take to transport me. Was I a "two-pack" or a "four-pack?" Would I even be found before the snow covered me and rendered me impossible to find? Would the wild beasts, in the end, get their payback and tear me to bits in the spring? Would they call it a *wild guide* dinner?

I was having trouble maintaining consciousness as each second inched along. After three days alone staring at a white world, even crazy ideas helped some to keep me awake. Mercifully, my mind returned to saner thoughts and I began to ponder my plight if somehow I was rescued. Upon arrival back at the lodge, the law was waiting to charge me with a felony, to take my career and freedom away, to charge me with a crime of which I honestly felt I was innocent.

Hooper would cheerfully handcuff me and do his best to destroy my life. Had someone worked with him to set me up? Again I felt a sense of helplessness, and deep inside I was starting to come to a crossroads in my heart. I knew I had to make a choice and soon, either to get angry enough to survive or to give up and die.

My thoughts drifted to my family. My wife was extraordinarily beautiful to me, and I wasn't sure she ever fully understood my need to be in the profession I had chosen.

She was in California and I could just imagine her lounging by a pool or on the beach in the hot sun while I was freezing. What a different world, yet a world that was part of me a few months of the year. I wondered what she was thinking, or if she was concerned about me. I did not always confide in her some of the narrow escapes because I did not want to cause her to worry when I was away in the wild.

I ground my teeth with the realization that another man might replace me in her life. What a special gift that would be for him! And solely because I was an idiot who liked to live on the edge. Would she think it served me right? Would my daughters miss their dad? These thoughts and possible answers to unspoken questions began to depress me, so I forced myself to think of other things. I have been told that depression is merely *anger without energy*, so I sensed I needed to energize my anger, and I knew just whom to think about to get the juices flowing. I began to vent mentally on Hooper.

Even so, I kept falling asleep and waking with a start, fearful that I had missed the plane I hoped would come for me. It was getting late in the afternoon (according to my watch), and I dreaded nightfall. I did not know if my body would survive to see the next dawn. I knew it was generating less and less heat. Thankfully, the weather had calmed a little and my hopes began to grow.

They grew even more when I thought I heard the drone of a small plane engine. I tried to listen intently and hone in on the sound. Yes. There it was again. I was not dreaming. It was faint but seemed to be getting louder. I struggled to my feet, hope energizing my cold frame. I strained my eyes in the direction of the noise. It got louder and louder. Someone was coming for me! Oh, please, let it be someone coming for me.

Then, miraculously, I saw the small outline of a plane just visible through the clouds and snowfall. I waved my arms and somehow found the strength to jump up and down, trying to holler through my chattering teeth and chapped lips. Then I saw the confirmation: The plane gave a waggle of its wings and I was ecstatic.

He had seen me! I recognized the plane and knew who the pilot was. It was Dave Wilder, and I could not believe he had found me. He circled a couple of times and we both knew this landing could be deadly in the undefined snow. After some time, he gave it a go, went sideways when his wheels hit the surface, began tilting dangerously, but managed somehow to stay upright and eventually came to a halt just a few yards from me. Miraculously, the modified wide "slick" tires he had installed on his 180 Cessna held up in the soft snow. It was unbelievable. To this day, it is the prettiest plane I have ever seen.

I just stood there shaking and staring, almost in disbelief, and not moving. An icicle is so hard and brittle that when it falls, it shatters into bits. I was so stiff, frozen and trembling with excitement that I felt that if I fell I might break into pieces too.

Dave opened the door and yelled at me, "Get in, Rocky! Get in! We gotta hurry, we gotta go now!" I staggered forward still clutching the prized tent. I dove awkwardly into the plane and Dave pulled me in far enough to close the door. He did not wait for me to secure myself. He immediately gunned his engine, swung the plane into the wind and blasted off, blowing snow in every direction. I was unable to see a thing and don't know how he could, but we began to lift off and soar into the white sky, into safety and away from my icy tomb. I was still numb but I was thrilled to be going to the lodge and happy beyond words to be going somewhere warm.

The noise of the engine and urgency Dave was exhibiting precluded chatting with him. I was very curious to know what and who awaited me at the lodge, but I knew Dave was concerned about getting back while the weather was still moderately favorable and before it socked in again, before it would make the airstrip at the lodge too treacherous to land on and before his windows, prop and engine iced up. He had risked his life to save mine and wanted a successful conclusion as much as I did.

Life and warmth began to surge back into my chilled body. Dave radioed ahead that we were en route and joyful congratulations were exchanged. By the time we arrived in the sky over the lodge, I was getting some feeling back into my legs and feet. That was a good thing because I wanted to walk with head high and exhibit a steady stride when I faced Hooper.

The weather was marginal and the snowfall created low visibility, but Dave circled and landed that snow-packed plane on the runway as if it were a clear sunny day. What an awesome pilot. We skated some and then taxied to a stop in front of the hangar. I peeked out of the frosty plane window and needless to say, I could just make out the form of Hooper, in full uniform, leaning confidently against the doorway frame, his right hand on his hip and a smirk on his face.

I exited the plane and thanked Dave profusely for his daring rescue. He just shrugged it off, but we both knew he had saved my life. Then I turned to face Hooper and learn what the rest of my life was going to look like. I walked toward him feigning confidence and innocence. That was easy, because in my heart, I believed I was.

As I drew closer to him, he straightened up and stepped toward me. He had a big grin on his face. He snarled, "I knew I was going to get you, Rocky! I knew it. I told you I was going to pull your ticket. Now give me your guide license!" I looked at him, showing a total lack of concern, and said mildly, "What in the world are you talking about, Hooper?"

He chuckled and replied, "Ha! Don't play dumb with me, Rocky. You are being charged with wanton waste. You left two caribou in the field. They were left on an inaccessible ridge and weren't packed out, but the horns are right here. I own you now!" He continued, "Now give me your guide license and when the arrest warrant comes through, I am going to take you in!"

I dutifully gave him the license and felt scared deep inside. What could I do? Who would believe me? Then I noticed Neon standing quietly in the corner a few feet away and taking this all in. With a quick jerking motion of his head, he directed me toward the "john" and then immediately disappeared. After a few moments, I made my way there as well. He grabbed me as I entered and whispered urgently, "Rock, I got my plane already warmed up and ready. Meet me ASAP right behind my cabin." I nodded and he exited quickly. I took care of business and then slipped through the woods to his cabin.

Within minutes, we were airborne again and headed back to the Nushagak Hills. God must love innocent people, because the weather actually cooperated and cleared up some as we raced back to the two caribou. I asked Neon if he could land in the snow on that ridge. He grinned broadly and said, "Just watch me. What do those guys know, saying a plane couldn't land there?"

We arrived and I gripped the door handle of the plane tightly as Neon maneuvered skillfully for his approach. He wasted no time and nailed it, skidding to within mere feet of the still frozen caribou. Had the weather not cooperated, of course, we would never have been able to find the caribou, much less land the plane. That is what made Wilder's landing so incredible. He had been flying blind while the wind and snow were still fuming. In my mind, he had flown with the eyes of God directing him.

Neon looked at me as we sat for a moment in his plane, parallel to the caribou. He laughed and chortled, "Can't land here, eh? Inaccessible, eh? Heck! Not only did I land here, but I did it in terrible conditions." Ah, it was nice to have a friend right now. We jumped out and loaded the caribou as fast as we could. I noticed that one shoulder had been ripped apart good, probably by a bear or wolf. I hoped not too much meat was lost. It would be truly depressing if I couldn't make the 143-pound weight requirement due to that, and I knew Hooper would give me no slack.

Chapter Four – Wilder to the Rescue

God was good and the weather stayed calm. We lifted off and headed back to the lodge. Neon tried to land as softly as possible, and then quietly allowed the plane to coast up to the hangar where the racks and the other caribou were. We rapidly unloaded the meat and set it beside their respective horns. We had just finished when I saw a flash of Hooper's uniform through the window. Neon ran out a side exit unnoticed, hurried to his plane and began the process of securing it. I stood near the caribou with a bland expression and pretended that all was well with the world. Meanwhile, my heart was pounding.

Hooper rounded the corner, strode directly at me, heels clacking on the cold wooden floor, and began yelling, "What are you doing, Rocky? You know that stuff is evidence. You better not mess with it!" He reached the location where all the caribou and horns were. All of a sudden, he stopped dead in his tracks and his mouth dropped open.

He looked at me and spat out accusingly, "So where did these come from, Rocky? What are you trying to pull? Did someone loan these to you?"

I was in no hurry. I gave him a sardonic smile and said softly, forcing him to lean in close to hear me, "Why, Hooper, these came from that inaccessible ridge that your buddies said a plane couldn't land on. I gotta be honest, Hoop, my grandmother could have landed on that ridge and she is 90 years old!" Hooper started to sputter something and then stopped, his eyes blazing at me. I wasted no time. I wanted to catch him while he was off guard.

I continued sweetly, "Let's see now. Three sets of horns and three caribou all properly tagged and bagged. I believe all is in order. Just what else do you require, Trooper Hooper?" I drew out this last part rather rhythmically. Hooper pressed his lips together tightly but couldn't help moving them back and forth. I knew he was gnashing his teeth. His breathing pattern was getting shorter and he was staring hard at the meat.

He then grunted, "Oh, yeah! Let's see if they make weight!" Dang, I was afraid of that. A bear or wolves had gotten a lot of that one shoulder. I replied confidently, "Go ahead, sir, and if I may ask, will you need any assistance lifting any of these heavy pieces?" He just glared at me and began weighing out the caribou portions.

The undamaged one came in easily over the 143-pound requirement. Then Hooper saw that the shoulder was damaged on the other one. I could almost see a faint smile creep onto his face. He grabbed the sections and began weighing them. I moved closer to watch the scales. I didn't want any fudging on his part.

When he had placed all the meat on the scales, he stepped back and I could tell he expected the weight to be light. We both intently waited as the scale settled down on a number. I felt my breath expel when I saw it stop squarely on the 143-pound mark. I looked at Hooper and gave him a huge smile. He glared at me a moment, then extracted the guide license from his pocket. With a flourish, he tossed it on the floor in front of me. He eyed me evenly and said, "Don't worry, Rocky. I will get you yet!"

I glanced over his shoulder and saw the grinning face of Neon standing outside. He gave me a thumbs-up and disappeared. I couldn't help myself. I gave Hooper one last parting shot. I said, "Hooper, you didn't mention whether you still wanted that caribou sausage. I think I still have some that isn't too spicy, cuz I would hate for anything to upset your stomach." His eyes bulged open and then he let me have it verbally. I won't repeat what he said, but frankly, it was music to my ears.

I slept like a baby that night, knowing that I was alive and free, knowing that I would soon be going back to my wife and girls, and I was especially glad that I was never going to let another man take my place in their lives!

A welcome sight when alone in the wilds. A bush plane coming to pick you up!

Chapter Five

Super Bowl Week

"Never buy jewelry from someone who is out of breath."

"**D**ad, this preacher is awful Why are you taking notes?" I whispered to him from a back pew of the musty little church in which 38 brave souls were trapped, half of whom were asleep while the others vainly tried to listen intently. Dad would dutifully scribble down hieroglyphic-like comments (illegible to anyone but himself) on yellowed 3x5 cards for each speaker. He would then file the cards away in those ugly rectangular, green boxes, and I suspected they were unlikely ever to be seen again.

Dad frowned and said, "Rocky, if you look deep enough you can find something good in everyone. Be quiet and pay attention. He might say something useful." *Yeah, when cows fly*, I almost muttered. Say, how about the Grand Canyon, I wanted to reply. Would that be deep enough for this guy?

Sorry, Dad, I didn't find any redeeming remarks in that speech. However, I have since discovered the wisdom in trying to uncover the hidden nuggets of treasure to be found in those with whom I come in contact. I almost make it a game, a very useful device to unravel and understand. Yes, it may take patience and a bit of digging with some, but it amuses me when I uncover some tucked-away talent or trait that their lives and troubles may have buried.

I see the person in a completely new light and develop a better comprehension of who they really are. The wilderness facilitates this exercise for me; it has a way of unwrapping irrelevant layers and allowing people to get back to simplicity, back to a more real person in touch with those things created with love for mankind. The farther and more remote they place themselves inside the wilderness, I believe the greater are their chances of contact with an untouched environment whose divine purity will richly touch their hearts.

Then, of course, there are those from whom talent just oozes, no matter how they may disguise it. Much like a beautiful lady trying to "dress down," and yet her loveliness still overwhelms, some simply exude strength, vitality and confidence with every step they take.

Such were the guests during this upcoming tumultuous week. Jeff Hostetler was a premier NFL quarterback and had one of the top career QB ratings of all time. He was, to put it simply, a stud. He had brought along his brother Doug and his father, Jeff Sr., for a special trip in the wilds. They were family, but they were also tight friends and very close.

"Hoss," as he is affectionately known, was born in Hollsopple, Pennsylvania. In college, he originally played for the legendary Joe Paterno at Penn State, but the team went in a different direction and Hoss transferred to West Virginia, where he immediately became a major star.

In his first game he tossed four touchdowns, and the Mountaineers shocked the top-ten ranked Oklahoma Sooners. Later in the same year, they beat another top-ten ranked team, the Maryland Terrapins, who were led by the legendary quarterback Boomer Esiason. Hoss was later inducted into the West Virginia Hall of Fame.

Hoss was drafted into the NFL by the New York Giants, but used sparingly for several years because Phil Simms, a terrific quarterback himself, was already directing the team and they won the 1986 Super Bowl. Hoss worked hard, maintained a good attitude and kept himself ready. His diligence paid off in late 1990. During the 14th game of the season, Simms was injured and Hoss stepped in.

Up until this time, Hoss had thrown a total of 109 career passes. So what did he do? He led the team to wins in their final two regular season games and then swept all comers in the playoffs, culminating in a Super Bowl victory over the Buffalo Bills in January 1991. He was a 4-1 in playoffs with an astounding 112 QB rating. He nearly took the Raiders to the Super Bowl as well. When his time came, he was ready.

When I met his group, I knew they were ready to hunt. They were in good physical condition, had great gear and were excited about the prospect of going out to a remote campsite, being dropped off and spending a week hunting caribou and swapping stories. In a way, this trip was a belated celebration of the Super Bowl win. What a great idea and setting for that purpose.

I had two other groups, and one was a husband and wife team. I asked hubby, "Who usually leads when you hunt together?" He squared up and said, "I do. I am the leader." I said, "Well, I will pray that your marriage is good, especially if your wife is going to be behind you in remote Alaska with no witnesses and a loaded rifle." They both looked at me and cracked up. (I was only half joking.) After all, the longest sentence one can form with two words is "I do."

I set up the three camps on the backside of Yellowstone Mountain, three to five miles apart, in an area where I had seen thousands of caribou in years past. Next day was opening day, and often the trophy bulls are still hanging with the herds. On the way in we spotted some large groups of caribou, and the excitement in the camps was enormous, especially when throughout the rest of the day a number of caribou trotted right by their tents.

When the caribou are plentiful, the toughest task a guide has is that of selection. "Hey, that's the biggest 'bou!" The guide will point frantically at a trophy animal and hope his client isn't so excited that they can't focus.

This year I had brought in a top-notch guide and packer for Hoss, and also to help me with what I anticipated would be a busy few days processing and packing out caribou to the few landing sites that we were able to mark on nearby ridges for our pilot. The guide's name was

Corey Collins. Corey was from Canada and had guided and packed with me for two years. He was really looking forward to working with the Hostetler group and meeting Jeff.

No one in any of the camps slept much that night, especially initially, and so they stayed up anxiously whispering to each other about the next day's hunt and discussing the best strategy. When dawn broke they were all up, tingling with anticipation, and quickly on their way. The air was crisp and cool, but no matter; they were hot to hunt.

Jeff's group had already devised a game plan and they were following it play by play. They hid below the skyline as they hiked, being careful to keep their profile low, and managed to place themselves in a terrific elevated vantage point surveying a large herd of caribou, which were completely unaware of their presence. As Jeff scanned the animals, his jaw dropped. He couldn't believe how big this one bull was. Corey was amazed too. It was the largest caribou that had been spotted by any of us in many years.

Jeff quietly controlled his breathing, took careful aim and BAM! He knew immediately he had hit the monster 'bou, but that bull was big and tough for a reason. Sort of like Jeff himself, who had been pummeled repeatedly by some massive NFL linemen bent on his destruction; yet Jeff proved to be rugged and had a reputation of never quitting. As you would expect, this 'bou did not quit or go down, but instead high-tailed it outta there. It began running downhill straight toward some makeshift dwellings in the distance.

Jeff was in hot pursuit. Hey, this guy could run! I checked later and discovered he had scored 17 touchdowns running the ball; pretty good stuff for a QB. As he steadily followed the 'bou, his hopes grew because he noticed it was slowing down. The problem, though, was that it was slowing down as it neared the temporary man-made site.

As it turned out, a young man had been watching and saw the 'bou coming his way. He had gotten his gun and hidden in a good position for his own ambush of the wounded and noticeably limping animal. Jeff was closing in, getting ready to finish off this trophy, when unexpectedly he heard a loud report in front of him and saw the caribou crash to the ground.

To Jeff's dismay, someone else had downed the 'bou. Figuring that whoever had shot simply didn't realize the 'bou was his, Jeff quickly un-chambered his rifle and ran to where the animal had fallen. When he arrived, he looked at it in amazement, dumbfounded at how big it was. It was truly a magnificent creature.

Jeff became aware of a man wearing a droopy hat, with messy black hair hanging over his ears and holding a rifle at the ready position. He was glaring at Jeff with dark, somber eyes and standing on the other side of the caribou in a clearly confrontational and possessive manner. Jeff sensed, like a blitz from his blind side, that a number of other people were starting to arrive, so he pointed at the caribou with his free hand and said loudly, "That's my caribou!"

Whoa! If Jeff was expecting understanding, cooperation or sympathy, he had ventured into the wrong spider web. None of his fans lived here, and who he was didn't matter a bear scat to the young, intense man standing near the caribou and sporting a derisive grin. The man began cursing at Jeff, vigorously. He started aimlessly waving the barrel of his gun in Jeff's direction.

After the hailstorm of curse words, the youngster paused, jutted out his jaw, curled his upper lip and growled, "I am from Alaska and I can see you ain't, so get the ___ off of my place!" Jeff smartly realized he had no sidelines to stop interlopers, no impartial referees to intervene and no coach's challenges available out here. This was the enemy's locker room; he was an intruder and this was getting serious, fast.

Jeff hesitated, wondering how things had spiraled out of control so quickly. He knew he would risk his body for the Lombardi Trophy, but he sure as heck wasn't going to put his life on the line for a dead caribou. He glanced casually to the sides and behind him, looking for a safe exit.

On the alert, he noticed that the barrel of the man's gun seem to be pointing more and more steadily at him—at his head, in fact. Jeff had no bullets in the firing chamber of his rifle and realized it would take too long for him to arm his gun if it came to that. He understood with crystal clarity that any misstep could be fatal.

His hesitation seemed to embolden the man. Jeff's focus sharpened and he saw the man's stringy black hair glistening from the sunlight and dark eyes flashing like glowing coals. The man shook his head, pushed his rifle in front of him and yelled, "You get the ___ outta here before I shoot your ever-loving ___. Ain't no crime cuz you are on my land."

Even as he was being yelled at, Jeff was prudently easing back and putting distance between himself and the group of onlookers. He felt his adrenaline surge as he noticed that the man was raising his gun. Just as Jeff was about to whirl and dash for cover, he realized that the man was lifting the gun in order to get the gun strap off his shoulder.

As soon as this was accomplished, the man dropped the gun down by his side and began shaking his head up and down, muttering, "Yeah, that's right. Get outta here and don't come back, punk." Jeff inwardly cringed because he was not one to back down from a challenge to his manhood, but another more prudent side of him heaved a sigh of relief. There was nothing to be gained or proved by being macho here. But he fully agreed with the man on one point: He was not ever planning to return.

Jeff continued to walk slowly backwards, grateful that years of backing up from the center to pass the football, often under extreme pressure, made this process second nature. With each step, his feelings of safety and confidence grew. He looked around quickly and noticed that this was a very roughshod dwelling site, haphazardly put together, and not surprisingly, there were a number of rather unkempt and rough looking characters lounging about.

It was obviously a different culture and they had their own code. Wisely, Jeff decided not to challenge it. You see, Jeff was also an *academic* all-American.

At last, Jeff was far enough away that he felt safe enough to turn around. Before he did, he took one last lingering look at his caribou. What a tremendous set of antlers. Hopefully he could find another one to match, but he knew that was a longer shot than Harvard winning the national collegiate football championship again. (It's true; they've won it several times, but the last one was in 1919.)

Jeff, his brother and his father did indeed harvest three very nice caribou. None approached the size of the one Jeff had lost, but the men were delighted nonetheless. A pilot flew over the camp, and even from the air, he could tell that Jeff's stolen caribou was special. It would have scored very high in the Gold Safari Club.

The other groups had animals down, too, totaling eight. The fun was over and my work began in earnest. Since I had a great packer in Corey, the idea was for him to process one set of four most nearly located to each other and for me to do the same with the other four, which were also somewhat geographically bunched. As I said, that was the idea . . .

Many of the animals were miles apart. In spite of that, I knew Corey and I could clean, cut up, bag and pack our designated animals to the appropriate landing site by the following evening. I knew that—until I got a desperate radio call.

When someone who is at the top of their profession is in attendance, people want to shine for them. I am sure Tiger Woods just shakes his head at many of his amateur partners who flail away mightily at the golf ball. Then, on those rare occasions when they connect solidly and power it down the fairway a whole 200 yards, they stop proudly, stand a little taller and slyly glance sideways at Tiger for approval. I'll bet he must chuckle to himself a lot.

Corey could see the gifted strength and power that Jeff possessed. Corey had chosen to process Jeff's animal first, and since this was a fully guided hunt, the clients are not supposed to nor expected to join in the work. That is why they pay the big bucks, so that the guides and I will do that for them. Corey was pretty strong, too, and as we macho men tend to do sometimes, Corey had decided that he wanted to impress Jeff and his group with his own prowess.

Corey versus Rockstar

Maybe he was thinking about the past year, when he and I had been guiding hunters at the end of the season. Our hunting season can be long and cold, particularly when you are hunting the entire time and don't get any significant relief. Normally, each client is there for one week, and then only two or three days at most are actually spent in the wilds before they are successful. Sometimes it is longer, but in all cases, they are back at the warm lodge within a week, soaking in a hot shower, enjoying the grub and telling tall tales.

The guides and I, however, are out in drop camps week after increasingly colder week, with winter freeze settling in and the grind a real struggle. When the last animals are down and you know that this will be your last pack for the year, you are filled with a surge of energy. The warm lodge, hot shower, clean clothes and hot food beckon. Even better, you know that within days you will be with your wife, your family surrounding you, with the knowledge that it will be another year before it begins again.

Corey and I stood there looking at the last two caribou for the season. It was our last pack. They were decent sized but not overwhelmingly large. Once we got these two bagged and tagged and to the landing site for the plane to pick up, we were done, vamoose, outta here for the year. I did not want to make two packs. I said, "Corey, I don't want to walk back. Let's pack a whole caribou each!"

Corey stiffened, looked at me to see if I was joking, and seeing that I was serious, gritted his teeth and grunted, "If you can do it, I can." A whole caribou in packing terms consists of four quarters, the tenderloins, back-strap, horns and, if the client chooses, the cape. Including our weapons, this would amount to an unwieldy load of over 200 pounds per person, traversing over a mile in rough terrain and through icy snow. What was I thinking?

After some creative tie-downs and adjustments to our packs, we eventually had them fully loaded. We laid the packs out, meat-side toward the ground, and then laid ourselves down with our backs on top of the packs. We cinched them firmly to our shoulders and upper bodies, rolled over onto our stomachs, worked our bodies up to a four-point stance onto our hands and knees and, with a little assistance from each other, slowly stood up.

We grabbed our rifles, which we had previously propped up because there was no way we could bend down to retrieve anything low. Whew! This was an awkward pack. I was determined not to show any weakness to Corey and resolutely began walking. He glanced at me, fought to get his balance and said rather too cheerfully, "Hey, Rock, this isn't as bad as I thought. How you doin', ole man?" He dragged out the "doin'" in the manner of an Italian mobster movie.

How was I doin'? Ole man? Other than a creaky back, bad knees, hearing loss and a thinning hairline, I felt great. I was coming to the opinion that this middle-aged youngish man (that being me) was an idiot. This bloody pack was heavy and I was finding it difficult to maintain my balance on the slippery terrain. I replied in what I hoped was a confident voice, holding my breath a little so as not to let him see how badly I needed air, "I'm just fine, Corey." Then, to spice this whole thing up a bit, I continued boldly, "In fact, I will make a bet with you that I beat you back to the landing site!"

What had I just said? Ouch. Too late to take it back now! My legs were beginning to burn. Maybe Corey would understand that I was only kidding and would not take me up on it. "You're on, big guy!" he retorted promptly. So much for Corey not accepting my silly offer. Okay, well, I wasn't going to go down without a fight; I needed a strategy.

Naturally, Corey sped up and soon had a few dozen yards on me. I kept thinking to myself, *Tortoise and hare, tortoise and hare. Just stay steady, big guy. Let him wear himself out.* We continued on this way for over a mile, and my body was screaming for a break. I knew neither of us could afford that because once we sat down, we would never make it back up and would have to split up our packs and make two trips, negating the entire purpose.

I noticed, though, that my steady pace was paying dividends. Corey was seemingly being pulled back to me by an invisible force. At last we were even, but I was exhausted and I knew that I needed a shot of adrenaline immediately. I said, "Corey, since we are dead even, let's stop for a second and catch our breath." I knew he needed it as badly as I did.

He tried to hide his laborious breathing, but billowing white clouds of hot breath in the cool air were a dead giveaway for both of us. He glanced at me and said, "I don't really need to rest, Rockstar, but I am sure your ole bones need a break." As he finished he started to chuckle, but his heavy breathing cut that short. He had sarcastically tossed in my nickname for emphasis. By gum, if ever I had needed that shot of energy, I had it now.

We stopped, leaned forward carefully and braced ourselves by putting our arms out stiff with our hands against our knees. Our rifles were slung with the straps over one side of our packs. We stood there bent over, rifles and bodies swaying in the wind, taking big gulps of air and trying to regain some strength. I sucked in a huge breath and said sarcastically, "Hey, you young pup, there's about 400 yards left to the landing area and I will run the whole way." Dang, I just can't stop, can I? I kept rising up to the bait, just like a farm-raised trout.

Corey was startled at this challenge. After he caught his breath, he squinted his eyes at me and barked, "Rockstar, I don't think I have ever met anyone so full of . . ." At this he trailed off, because I was already off and running. He charged after me. Now, when I say running, I am using the term *very loosely*. In our minds, we were sailing along the terrain like snow leopards gliding over snowy ridges. In reality, we were stumbling and bumbling along more like turtles inching up a rocky incline.

Once again, Corey passed me and got a short lead. *Tortoise and hare, tortoise and hare.* Then, with about 100 yards to go, I saw him wavering. This gave me a shot of confidence, and I put all I had into that last stretch. With about 30 yards left, I passed him, and when I reached the landing site I fell forward to my knees, bent sideways and rolled over. I lay there gasping for air and was completely spent, but I had a big grin on my face. I had won! Take that, youngster. "Ole man" is alive and well. Rockstar ain't dead yet.

A Poor Choice

Maybe this past incident had a lot to do with what Corey did next in trying to impress Jeff Hostetler. Corey did not take into account several things, however. That previous pack was at the end of the year when his muscles and balance were at their peak, and that other caribou was not as large as Jeff's was. Corey had only been back for two days, so he really needed to start slowly.

Instead, on his first pack of the new season, he decided to duplicate what we had done at the end of last year. He was going to pack out Jeff's caribou in one load. Jeff was watching Corey closely and it dawned on him what Corey was doing. He asked Corey in alarm, "Are you going to pack out that whole caribou in one trip?" Corey replied, "Yep."

Jeff was very concerned. He had exercised with some terrific athletes. He knew a great deal about safety and injuries. He gave one last speech to Corey: "This is not a good idea. Please don't try it." Corey just grunted and said, "I can handle it." Jeff wasn't convinced. He implored Corey, "Hey, look, I know you are experienced and all, but I don't think you can do this. We aren't in that much of a hurry. Don't do it."

Funny how half-time speeches work wonders for the team with the best and smartest players . . .

Corey didn't heed Jeff's pleas. After he had the pack cinched up, he got down onto his knees and asked Jeff to help him load the pack, cape and horns onto his back. Jeff pleaded with him to reconsider, but Corey was adamant and so, grudgingly, Jeff obliged and helped him load the pack. Once that was accomplished, Jeff helped Corey stand up.

Jeff was convinced this was a terrible idea. He watched anxiously as Corey shifted his feet nervously and got his balance. At that point Corey seemed ready, and he rocked forward, took one halting step and collapsed, tumbling down in excruciating pain. Corey had blown out one of the lower lumbar discs in his back and was writhing on the ground.

Jeff rushed to his aid and removed the pack. Corey was in terrible shape, hurting badly, and couldn't walk. Jeff felt horrible for him, even more so because he could not understand why Corey had not heeded his advice. Here they were in wild, remote Alaska, far from any hospital or doctor, and Corey needed help fast.

They immediately called me on the radio, informed me of the awful news and told me that Corey was hurting terribly, couldn't walk and was immobilized. Corey needed emergency treatment ASAP. I quickly radioed for a plane to come in and pick him up. I was glad that our location was not far from our lodge and the plane arrived shortly.

We had to cradle Corey and gingerly carry him to the area where the plane landed. The plane left as soon as he was loaded, took him to the lodge, and from there we were able to arrange quick transportation to Anchorage for the care he needed.

I was bummed for Corey and I was in serious trouble without him. I had eight caribou down between the three groups, spread out over eight to ten miles, and no one to help me clean and pack them out. Beyond this immediate emergency, I had no seasoned guide on hand to be a packer for the next hunting parties that were coming. Life can certainly come at you fast.

There was one bright spot, however. I learned that the lady of the husband-wife team had also gotten a caribou and I was delighted for her. I asked her if her 'bou was bigger than her "leader's" 'bou. She winked slyly at me, then said sweetly, drawing it out, "Oh, no, his was *much* larger." Her husband raised his eyebrows and turned to look at me to see if I was buying it. I had to laugh at this, but I smiled even more when nine months later they called and happily told me that they had given birth to a son. That kid should have an adventurous spirit. After all, he had his beginnings in the remote wilderness of Alaska!

Well, I desperately did not want the animals to spoil. I hustled on foot to each site and cleaned them, inserting sticks to allow them to air out. Near several of the locations, I was able to find some pockets of leftover ice and snow that had not fully thawed during the summer. I scooped up handfuls of snow and placed as much as I could over and inside those animals. The caribou that were near the snow pockets, I dragged closer and tried burying them in the snow.

I don't know how many miles I covered before nightfall, but when I got to the last one, it felt like 15 or 20. Early the next morning, I returned to process the caribou and began the arduous task of packing them on foot to the nearest landing site. I knew I would not get to all the animals in time if I did this alone. I adroitly tried to suggest to one group, to whom I had given deeply discounted rates, that I could use some help. They said, "Rock, we aren't in shape for that and we would probably get hurt trying. We feel for you, man."

They had a point, and I certainly didn't want any of the guests being injured. I radioed to the lodge and asked them to fly out one of the fishing guides to help. He had never hunted with me or packed before. He was in for a quick initiation. He might have been green when we started, but he was fast becoming a seasoned pro by the time we finished.

Those three days of hiking and packing with a new fishing guide felt like three weeks. I lost count of how many miles I walked and how many packs we made. Late into moonlight on the third evening, we at long last, made our last pack. I knew I had done my best to save the meat. Several pilots rushed in and picked up the meat for transport.

If I have one bit of advice for young people, it is to know your limits and the situation, and always put safety first. Grandstanding is best suited for the playground and not a wise choice for the wilderness.

The young fishing guide was needed at the lodge and I was without a guide for upcoming clients. The pilot ferried all three groups to the lodge. Once there, they excitedly began fishing for trophy pike and salmon in the Holitna River, using my boats and fishing guides, telling stories and having a great time relaxing, eating wild game, enjoying homegrown Alaskan vegetables and catching a bunch of salmon.

I, however, was in a conundrum. In three days the next group would arrive, and I needed a packer pronto. For reasons I can't recall, I called up my buddy, Ken Ruettgers, who was due to come up soon himself. He had been another top NFL player, for the Green Bay Packers. He had fished and hunted with me a number of years and is truly a great guy.

Ken had been a star lineman for Green Bay for 12 years, a career much longer than most linemen had. He butted heads with outstanding linemen of his era and was a teammate of Brett Favre. During 1996, his 12th season, Ken blew out his knee and had to retire. At the end of that season, Green Bay won the Super Bowl.

Ken sat there watching the game and was thrilled that they won, but lost inside that he wasn't on the field with his teammates. I don't know if he received a Super Bowl ring, but if not, in my opinion, he darn well should have. It is ironic that an injury set the stage for Hostetler to win a Super Bowl, yet it was also an injury that stole one from Ken.

Ken was coaching football in Sisters, Oregon, so I probably hoped he knew of a strong, tough young man from his team whom I could hire who wanted to build up his strength and stamina during the off-season, or who had graduated and needed something to do. I figured that a rugged man like Ken could be counted on to know whether a young lad had the right stuff to work in the wilderness.

We chatted and then I asked, "Ken, I desperately need a strong kid to help me with the rest of hunting season as a guide and packer." Ken thought a minute and replied, "I have the perfect guy for you, Rocky. His name is Jacob." I responded  hopefully, "How old is he?" Ken said, "He is almost 18, Rock, and get this: He loves to fly." I said, "That's music to my ears, Ken; get him up here on the next plane!"

Tail–dragger landing on a gravel bar—An "E-Ticket" ride!

A great guide makes all the difference. On the left is Dr. James Leininger, called by some the "most influential Republican in Texas." He is a staunch conservative and man of deep faith. On the right is Marc Davis, my longtime friend and Alaskan Guide. My good friend "Jim" and his guide Marc were delighted with this Safari Club Trophy Rack.

Chapter Six

Wake-Up Call

His mom told me later that Jacob was obsessed about planes ever since he could walk. While other kids were playing with dump trucks and toy soldiers, Jacob was building balsa-wood airplanes.

He would frequently beg his mom to take him to the library so he could study pictures of planes. She would dutifully whisk her preschooler off to the library, where he would sit and study any pictures of planes that showed the instruments and the cockpits. Slowly and intently, he would go over each picture in detail, painstakingly memorizing all his mind could contain.

She figured this would be a passing fancy like the Pokémon phenomenon, but it wasn't. Her son was deeply passionate about his obsession, and his father told me later that they would be somewhere outside and Jacob would hear a plane going by and immediately stop and try to locate it in the sky. He would see the outline and recite the type of plane and a myriad of facts about it, or if he couldn't actually see it, he would often identify it just from the sounds the motor, prop or jet propulsion made.

He would tell you how high it was flying, the flight patterns and path, its speed and a host of other details so that soon you would be convinced he had built the darn thing just from the knowledge he proudly possessed. I guess you could say that Jacob was himself possessed. He was a "plane nut," and as I was later to learn about this quiet, intense young man, this was true in many ways.

As he grew older, Jacob worked hard at the construction job with his dad, but his heart wasn't in it. Jacob wanted to fly. He wanted to soar in the heavens and feel the awesome freedom and power of being swept along in the thin blue air high above the earth. He wanted to glide like a bald eagle, dart like a midnight bat and dive like a red-tailed hawk. The heavens were calling him.

When the call came from me about needing a guide in Alaska, it was an amazingly divine appointment for this young man. Alaska is the great frontier of bush pilots. There are more pilots and planes per  capita in Alaska than any state in the U.S., and probably more than any other place on earth. I doubt that there is a better place to learn the real art of flying, outside of dog fighting in wartime. I can't fathom a more apt or tougher training ground than Alaska.

Jacob had recently told his dad, "I don't want to work construction with you anymore, Father. I love you, but I am crazy about flying. I guess I'm saying that I want to find my own life, and to do that I need to be a pilot. So please don't be offended, Father, but I can't do that working construction."

I must say, what a cool dad. When Jacob asked him about accepting my offer to go to Alaska, his dad said, "Are you loco? Of course you are going. This is the opportunity you have always wanted. Go for it!" His dad then added, "If you don't go, I will!"

Jacob's father was Ken Ruettgers' best friend, and Jacob was an all-star state football player. He played fullback and middle linebacker—two very tough positions that required strength and guts. Ken, who knew Jacob very well, figured Jacob could hold up to the rigors of being an Alaskan guide for me. Ken had firsthand knowledge of how rugged Jacob really was. You see, Ken was Jacob's coach.

This was all the encouragement that Jacob needed, so he packed quickly and, just before leaving, stood nervously in front of his parents. His bags were full and he was going into the unknown. It was one thing to talk about going out into the world to find yourself. It was quite another to actually be taking the first step. Fantasy was edging toward reality.

Ken was there to say goodbye too. Ken had fished with me and had met my family. He was shrewdly aware of how beautiful the girls were and wondered if this might distract Jacob. He looked keenly at Jacob, furrowed his eyebrows tightly and asked him in a challenging tone, "What about Rocky's four beautiful daughters, Jacob? I happen to know they are charming, full of life and quite good looking."

Jacob never batted an eye. He looked back at Ken and answered the challenge in a firm voice, "Ken, one thing I do know and that is this: You never mess with the boss's daughters!"

Finding Your Way

Hey, I liked this guy already. When I heard of Jacob's other comments to his parents, I immediately reflected back on a similar time in my life when I wanted to find my own path.

I was a young man and lost in a world full of contradictions. One group said this, another touted that and I felt pulled in many directions. Most things that were fun were supposedly evil, and things that were extolled as beneficial and righteous appeared boring and dull. One of Dad's favorite quotes was from the late John R. Rice, and he said it often: "Do right even if the stars fall." That sounded mindless to me.

My Grandfather Joel was as tough as they come and renowned in many ways. He was short and sinewy with a quiet strength and force that made him seem much taller. He was feared and revered.

I used to stare at his gnarled hand, which had been bitten by a big rattlesnake. He had simply shaken the rascal loose, cut an X above the spot the fangs had pierced, sucked on it thoroughly and spit out the poison.

Grandmother Ethel was the jewel in his crown and a saint on earth. When she talked you would swear she had hard candy tucked in her cheek. She always had a twinkle in her eyes, contrasted with coal black hair lined with gray.

She was a Cajun and they married at 16. They raised 13 kids on a dirt farm, scratching out a living with home-grown crops, cows and chickens.

Chores consumed daylight hours and fights were common among the children, but in the end love and laughter held the upper hand. It was rumored that sometimes Joel resorted to his horsewhip on more than just his equines, but no matter; his kids revered him long after he died.

It was a hard life and rules were strict. Rebellion wasn't brooked and a parent's word was the law, to be obeyed without question. This was the climate my parents lived in and the path modeled for them. The South is the Bible Belt, and the Great Depression was more than a memory, it was a driving force. Kids were to be seen and not heard, and survival depended on loyalty to the leader of the home.

At the time, none of that connected with my generation. To us the Depression was but a footnote in history, the big war was over, the right guys had won and it was time to party. We wanted to play, seek out a new path and explore the technological advances, much like the kids of today. However, to our parents there was no gray. Everything was black and white.

Who decided what was right? I thought I had a good mind and if I viewed something a different way, who was to say I wasn't right at least once in awhile? Some of this stuff was open to different interpretations, I felt. I finally had enough and fled from home and wound up with an uncle whom I greatly admired who, ironically, lived in the Deep South. I had returned to my roots.

He had a booming voice and was big, tall, rich and full of life. To me, he was bigger than life, and he drove a sleek, beautiful Cadillac. Of course he did. He owned the dealership and the local bank. He lived in a 13-bedroom, 13-bath mansion on an expansive pecan plantation, complete with a private bass lake, and he even had an elevator inside his home.

Pretty snazzy when you recall this was rural Mississippi back in the 1960s. My uncle had jet-black slicked-back hair reminiscent of those gangsters you see on *The Untouchables,* and he had a snarl that would send a porcupine scooting. He lived as he drove, hard and fast. He also had a heart the size of Texas and I loved him.

He loved me, too, and when I ran, I eventually went to him. I saw him as successful, and I hoped he could help me clarify my own journey and sort out this puzzle called life that I and I'm sure many teenagers continue to struggle with today.

No matter the advances in technology, the underlying issues are basically the same as they have been from the time of Adam: Wanting control, cutting the ties and testing your mettle. Searching for meaning, finding a purpose and maybe even falling in love.

You probably have a similar story of those years in your life. Maybe your parents were clueless and inflexible and seemed too strict. Or possibly it was something else, but isn't it ironic how much softer, wiser and smarter they seem to have gotten since? (I can't wait until my kids discover the same about me.)

Well, when I landed in the South it was a tumultuous time. There were deep racial tensions, and integration was the conversation of the day. I had come from Alaska, a huge melting pot of humanity of all types, and these issues and concerns simply weren't mine. Partially because of this, I didn't fit in. I got into major fistfights and became a good brawler, usually holding my own. I began to relish seeking out anyone who wanted to take me down.

I often came dragging in late, bruised and battered with my clothes dirty and torn. Please don't misunderstand me as to my feelings about the South. Although Alaska is my first love and where I've hung my hat, heart and bunny boots for many years, I consider the South my second home and will always be drawn to it. I love the South passionately.

The Alaskan wilderness owns my soul and I would soon be back there, but during this time as a teenager, I was simply a kid from Alaska who really didn't understand or care about the Southern political climate. I didn't want to get involved. I had personal issues I had to sort out.

I eventually had it. Just before my 18th birthday, I decided I wanted to be free from everyone and go it alone. I was sick of rules, schools and religious fools. I wanted to test myself. I was looking for adventure and challenges far bigger than a fistfight with a local cowboy. As I thought about it, I tried to imagine what could be the most exciting life and job possible.

Then it hit me. Why not fight for real? Why not fight for another uncle—Uncle Sam? I made up my mind at that moment. I would join the Navy and become a PBR, a riverboat driver. I would stare death in the face and match myself against lousy odds on the infested rivers and in the dangerous jungles of Viet Nam.

Little did I know at the time that later in my career I would be driving the wild and crazy rivers in Alaska and that those scary dashes and clashes in the twisted rivers of Viet Nam would become an invaluable reference.

Once I made up my mind to join the Navy, it seemed so logical and clear. That is, until I tried to explain it to my aunt and uncle. They were horrified and protested loudly. They took away my car—a new Cadillac, no less—and most of my privileges. They just could not fathom why I would want to leave.

Looking back, I can see their point. I had it made. I had come from a poor background, yet with them I was living in the lap of luxury, driving a fancy car, provided pocket money to spend and college was fully paid for. They treated and loved me like the son they never had.

Ultimately one night, for reasons I can't recollect, it all came to a head. I was fed up with my life and lack of purpose. Picture water dripping slowly into an open, empty barrel. It inches its way excruciatingly slowly up to the rim. When the water level at length, reaches the rim, it seems to defy gravity and does not immediately spill. It bulges up above the rim until that last tiny droplet crashes into the surface and zap, the water spills over onto the ground.

The droplets of anger, bitterness and frustration had in the end, overwhelmed me and burst forth. I can recall the exact moment. It was about 6 p.m. I was at Pearl River Junior College and all at once, my emotions erupted. I had to get out of there, now.

I called my uncle and told him I was through with college and that I wanted him to pick me up. I wanted to go back to his house. I told him I was going to join the Navy. He and my aunt were devastated. They refused to come. They hoped I would change my mind. I waited but no one came.

I was wearing light clothing and penny loafers. Back then, before the freeways and new highways were built, it was over 13 miles of rough country roads from the college to my uncle's mansion. I had no one to take me there, so I set out walking. Each step strengthened my resolve.

It was during that long walk on a hot, dark, humid Mississippi night that I began an even greater journey. My feet started burning and began to bleed, my legs were aching and my head was pounding, but I only saw these as challenges. Each step was becoming more and more painful, but I was also taking huge steps toward manhood.

Bugs were everywhere and the night noises were deafening with the crickets, frogs, chickadees and other rustling sounds that made me nervous. In the humid air I started sweating profusely, soaking my clothes and socks, which were rubbing against my skin creating even more burning and irritation. I tried to ignore the pain by pretending I was in Viet Nam sneaking out from deep within enemy territory.

The hours crept by and I had a lot of time to reflect and contemplate life—my life. In due course, early in the morning I could faintly see the outline of the mansion up ahead. At that moment, something was happening inside of me, and I felt a chilling current of electricity run through me, energizing me. I had made it! I had challenged my body and it was hurting, but I had done it. I had ignored the pain. I knew then I was ready for more.

I was fully committed. I had heard of missionaries who had ridden boats to remote pagan islands, and then destroyed their boats because they planned to never return. I had begun a new journey. I was not going back.

When I arrived at the mansion, I sat on the porch for a few minutes and reveled in the sweet rest this provided my body. I quickly learned what a big mistake this was, because when I tried to stand up to open the door, I had become stiff and almost collapsed from the pain. This was a valuable lesson that probably saved my life later on those occasions in the Alaskan wilderness when I needed to keep moving, although my body was crying for just a few moments of rest.

My uncle had a wonderful compassionate black lady who worked many years for them as a maid. I adored her. We all did. She had a hearty laugh that made her whole body shake. Her name was Elsa and she met me at the door. The concern in her warm, brown eyes when she saw me was immensely touching. I am not sure, but I think she might have teared up.

She looked at my feet, shook her head sympathetically and murmured, "Ooh, child, what you gone done now? You just sit over here. Elsa will take care of you."

She hustled me into a soft chair, turned her face away quickly and hurried off to get homemade beignets covered with lots of powdered sugar, along with thick, hot, black coffee laced with chicory. No one could cook like she did. I can still taste those beignets. I felt life flowing back into my system. I had a crazy thought: This is why I will be fighting. I have a purpose now. Elsa was a free woman because her ancestors and brave soldiers had fought for her, and I would be fighting to keep others free.

I had just started in on my second beignet when my aunt and uncle came downstairs. They stood there a few moments glaring at me, taking in my sweaty, disheveled clothes, discarded dirty loafers and swollen feet. My uncle leaned on his cane with both hands, bent toward me and in time barked, "Well, boy, are you done with this foolishness?"

I looked up at him, the beignet arrested halfway to my lips, hating that this was going to hurt them, yet also having a silly thought about not spilling the powdered sugar all over, and said quietly, "No, sir, I am leaving. I am going to Viet Nam."

Oh, boy! He exploded. He reared up, his cane went flying, clattering along on the hardwood floor, and he bellowed something so loud I don't even know what language it was. I do know that I spilled coffee onto his expensive chair, and the half-eaten beignet tumbled into my lap with the white powder trailing behind it like little puffs of smoke.

That smoke was nothing to the smoke coming from my uncle. His booming voice was shaking the windows, and he was tottering without his cane. I was horrified, thinking he might fall. My frail aunt was in tears, clutching him tightly, and Elsa was wringing her hands in her apron and rocking from foot to foot in quick rhythm, back and forth.

After awhile it got quiet—so quiet, it was somewhat eerie after all the noise. I slowly got up, slipped on the beat-up loafers, looked at Elsa, mouthed "thank you" and started hobbling toward the door. My uncle followed me with his eyes and then asked abruptly, "Where do you think you are going?"

I didn't even pause, but said firmly, "I am going to the recruiting station. I am signing up today." I got to the door, exited with some difficulty and began walking down the stairs toward the street. I glanced back and saw my aunt peering anxiously out the window, her white hair in stark contrast to the dark interior; and Elsa standing at the door, her hands folded together like she was about to pray.

My uncle picked up his cane and hustled after me, limping with each step. He began talking rapidly, beating his cane on the ground, staccato fashion, punctuating each sentence. "Rocky, I know Pearl River is just a junior college, but I will send you to any four-year college you like. I will send you to law school, whatever you want. Please don't do this." I had never heard my uncle plead. It tore at my heart.

I just shook my head and continued up the long, endless driveway, walking toward the street. My body was either filled with adrenaline or loosening up for some other reason. Thankfully, I was becoming numb to the pain. I got to the street and turned toward town en route to the bus terminal. I knew I could take the bus to Jackson, Mississippi, where there was a recruiting station.

My uncle stopped in his driveway and began yelling for Timmy, a dedicated black man who worked for him and with whom I loved to fish. Timmy would patiently bait the hooks for my uncle and me. He was thin, had a wispy mustache and was always chuckling about something. Sometimes he would tell me stories. My uncle hollered, "Timmy, bring 'round my Cadillac. Hurry!"

Timmy did just that, and my uncle got into the passenger's side of the car. He told Timmy to drive up alongside of me as I was walking. I was on the right side of the road, so my uncle was right next to me. He rolled down the window and continued to try to stop me. He said,

"Boy, get in the car. We are going fishing! I got Timmy here."

He paused and waited. I continued walking toward town, head slightly down, stride resolute. He then started pleading. "Rocky, come on now, get in. We'll make everything right for you."

Timmy even chimed in: "Mister Rock, let's go fishing. I know where there are some big redfish out in the Gulf Coast. We will take JV's boat." I smiled ruefully to myself. I had no doubt that Timmy could deliver on his promise. But my mind was made up.

This sleek, black Cadillac and pedestrian procession continued for what seemed like a couple of miles, my uncle and Timmy alternately pleading with me, and me saying repeatedly, "I'm sorry, Uncle, but I can't do it. I need to go my own way."

I never quit walking and never got into the Cadillac. Lastly, with a huge sigh, my uncle dropped his head, put one hand over his eyes and ordered Timmy to turn around and go back home. My heart was heavy but I continued to walk. For some reason, the pain in my body began to return.

I reached the bus station and caught a bus to Jackson. I was directed to the recruitment office, and within an hour, I was sworn in. I wish I could say that I recall the proud moment I became a Navy man, but things were getting blurry by then. I had been up all night, walked almost 15 miles, endured a very emotional encounter with my wonderful aunt and uncle and now I was a sailor. Nothing seemed real and my body was crashing. A couple of hours later, I was put on another bus and sent to Orlando, Florida.

All I know is, that trip didn't last nearly long enough for me to get the rest my body craved. I remember only brief moments of sleep and then stumbling in the dark to a bunk in a dimly lit navy barracks and passing out—that is, for about five minutes.

The enemy had gotten me! I was being wrestled to the ground and shaken violently. I tried vainly to resist and then I heard someone shouting in my ear, "You better get your butt up, sailor! This here ain't the French Riviera. You with your long, blonde, curly hair thinking you are cute. I bet you're from California. And guess what, sailor— I hate people from California! Get your butt up NOW!"

California? What was he talking about? Who was from California? I was an Alaskan!

I tried to force my eyes open and comprehend what was happening. He had said "sailor." Oh, yes, that was it. I had been sworn in yesterday. Or was that a dream? Suddenly a blast of freezing water hit me in the face. It was a shock but the effect was immediate. I opened my eyes wide and looked around. All the other recruits were standing at the foot of their perfectly made beds, neatly dressed and at attention. I was the only one still in bed. Uh-oh, this could not be good.

No, it was not good at all. I had deftly managed, on the first day as a sailor, to incur the permanent wrath of the head drill sergeant in my section. I quickly tried to get to my feet, feeling all the pain of the last two days, barely able to stand. I was half-dressed. Where was my shirt? Was I supposed to salute? How did this work? I looked meekly at the sergeant, gave a weak salute and mumbled, "Sir, yes, sir!"

He became even madder. I could see his neck veins bulging. He sputtered, "I ain't no officer, slick!" He started shouting so hard spit was coming out of his mouth and splattering all over me. I remember him yelling the following phrase with his nose pushed right up against mine, "You better give your heart to Jesus, son, cuz your behind belongs to me!"

I could see some of the other recruits snickering, and all I knew to do was to stand as tall and still as I could. *Maybe I should have listened to my uncle*, I was regretfully thinking. What the devil had I gotten into? Had I traded one taskmaster for an even bigger one?

That day was one of the longest and rudest awakenings I ever had. It was a blur of yelling, screaming, my hair being whacked off, running, quick-step, quick dressing, getting clothes that didn't fit, shining shoes and a nap somewhere that was entirely too short. Oh, and standing in lines forever to be served food that sucked.

What an idiot I was. I thought I was running away from rules. Becoming my own man. All of a sudden I was faced with more regulations and senseless tasks than I had ever imagined possible. My bed had to have perfect hospital corners, clothes put on just so, gig line, shoes spit shined, standing at attention for days in the hot, humid sun, push-ups by the thousands, it seemed—and marching.

Did I mention marching? We marched from dawn until dusk. I marched in my dreams. I marched in the shower. I marched to the toilet. I marched to breakfast, lunch and dinner. I marched and marched until my feet were screaming even louder than the cranky, nasty, cigar smoking, tobacco spitting, foul-breathed drill sergeant, who gleefully pursued his personal vendetta against me the entire time I was there.

Even today, when someone yells, "Hut two," I jump up and fall into step. Sometimes when I am deep in my Alaskan wilderness home hiking a hidden trail, I feel as if I am still marching . . .

Ah, but with each step that I marched, I was continuing my journey into manhood, toward finding my inner self, a path that eventually led to the Alaskan wilderness. I had finally begun my own bumpy rite of passage.

Jacob's Path

I smiled to myself and my mind returned to Jacob, who also had rejected a surefire future and wanted to march to the beat of his personal drum, to travel his own trail.

I could not help but be drawn to him, to feel a kindred spirit. Jacob was intent on being a pilot. He believed he was born to fly. Would he crash or would he truly soar and fly?

He wanted to explore his passion in the Alaskan wilderness, a wilderness tougher than any drill sergeant, harsher than any parent or lawman. Truly, this untamed wild frontier could kill him or destroy him in so many ways. But I knew from personal experience that this wilderness and the adventures he would face here could also make him a man.

Chapter Seven

Quest for Manhood

"Born to Fly"

One day he was hammering nails, and the next Jacob was on a big jet en route to Anchorage, Alaska. There he climbed aboard a much smaller aircraft and was flown to Lake Clark, where he then boarded a very small bush plane to be flown to the lodge. Each part of the trip whetted his appetite for more. He was in absolute heaven, literally, figuratively and emotionally. As each plane got smaller, his excitement got bigger. He knew he had made the right decision.

He had arrived in the land of bush planes and pilots. He felt like a cat at Microsoft: Mice everywhere, but how do you connect? Jacob was thrilled at the opportunity to see bush pilots up close, and he couldn't wait to fly with one of them. He hoped someone would give him that chance, and soon.

He had heard many stories from Ken about the bush pilots and the dangers of flying in the wilderness. There is no better place to challenge oneself as a pilot than in the Alaskan bush. Jacob could hardly sleep knowing he would soon be experiencing this for himself up close, and maybe even have the opportunity to fly a bush plane himself.

Flying was his ultimate dream. His parents had given him flying lessons in well-maintained planes at safe airports with good instructors, and he had easily excelled because of his talent and passion, but this was a far different kettle of fish. Jacob wanted to fly here, but knew he would have to prove himself first.

I watched him carefully after he arrived. Ken had told me a lot and I was curious. I saw that Jacob had good size, was in great shape and was very strong. Although almost 18, he seemed naïve and this suggested a sheltered upbringing. I was totally okay with that because I suspected he had been raised with a great set of values and had not developed any bad vices.

Happily, I discovered he was quiet, possessed great manners and was a very good worker. Along with that, he was reliable and had good habits. I had a sense early on that he would excel in this endeavor, and I had a notion almost from the time I met him that if he did, I would be willing to put some resources into him.

Of course, he wasn't without some odd habits too. Talk about set routines. This guy brushed his teeth the same number of strokes every dang time. How do I know? *He counted them aloud!. . .* 99, 100. It was enough to drive you batty. I wanted to grab his arm and force him to take one more stroke. Oh, but there was more. He put on his clothes the same way each morning. He was organized to the point of being anal and never deviated from his routines.

I mean, talk about a daily ritual. This fellow would sit exactly the same way in the same place at the same time, then make his logbook entries in the exact same manner each day, angle his face just so, and do this for every blasted task! I took to moving his chair and logbook, messing up his clothes, anything for my own sanity, just to vary his routine. Nevertheless, I will give him this: He was good at handling any changes I created and rarely got upset.

I once spent about a month with Jacob out in remote spike camps, guiding and packing for a season of hunters. I must tell you, being in that close proximity with another person makes it hard to hide those little set ways all of us develop. Well, after that month of being painfully aware of monsieur Jacob's funky traits, I was driven into heavy counseling for months . . . Well, almost.

During the time I got to know him, I sensed a deep inner resolve in Jacob, a quiet strength from a person who did not try to impress anyone. He knew what he wanted and he wasn't going to let anything interfere. And his plans fit right in with mine. He wanted to be a pilot and I always needed good pilots. I was willing to put some money into this guy and hoped he would fly my planes someday. I was willing to do that because he and I both wanted the same thing, with no side trips, hopefully.

He fit right in with my family. He liked to play Balderdash or Nerts, and usually partnered with my second oldest daughter, Merilee. Seeing him play some of these family games with our girls was the first time we saw him act vivacious and come alive. It was also when his competitive juices would start flowing. *Just remember, Jacob, you don't mess with the boss's daughters!*

Sure enough, just as he had hoped, Jacob was in for a treat. Within the first couple of weeks, Joel and Jeremy, both outstanding bush pilots who flew for me on occasion, checked Jacob out on the tail wheeler (so named because of the third wheel that is under the tail). Of course, this was my prize Super Cub. I had some anxious moments, but Jacob did quite well and Joel and Jeremy were impressed with his start, and it is not easy to impress these guys. They have seen it all.

As he continued to go on flights with Joel and Jeremy, they were amazed at Jacob's natural ability. They told me to check him out, so I watched him do "touch-and-goes" off the airstrip, and then in the field I saw him land on hillsides and stop in a very short space, nearly equal to the veteran pilots. I got goose bumps watching him. I knew in my heart, this young man was indeed born to fly.

After awhile, I began to let Jacob fly baggage haul and non-occupancy flights. He wasn't certified to fly people in the bush at this stage, no matter how many thousands of hours he may have logged in the Lower 48. The rules in Alaska are strict, and they need to be. Five hundred documented hours of specific Alaska bush flying is required for certification in order to be insurable to carry passengers.

Consider this: Every 2,000 hours that a bush plane engine is flown, it has to undergo what amounts to a complete overhaul to be recertified. Planes like the Cessna Super Cub haven't been manufactured in years, and the FAA is extremely tough on compliance. Due to rough usage conditions in Alaska, on average these bush planes are refurbished or rebuilt every seven years. To keep them certified and safe, they are essentially rebuilt over and over.

A complete overhaul pretty much amounts to a new engine and virtually a new plane. It is very different from a tune-up on your car. Often, the price tag can be thirty to fifty thousand dollars.

Gas in Alaska is far higher than in the States, although I don't understand why, since we produce so much from the North Slope. Can someone explain why that same gas, processed and shipped from Alaska to Arizona, costs less there than in Alaska?

AV gas (aviation gas) can cost up to $10 a gallon especially with the extra expense to get it flown in to the lodge, and conservatively, the cost of flying a plane is $250 to $350 an hour. Of course, Jacob was an employee who had other jobs to do as well. What it all boils down to is that for him to qualify on the planes and rack up 500 hours was a very expensive proposition for me.

Not surprisingly, a plane that has logged little of the 2,000 hours available has a correspondingly higher value, so flying a plane more hours, even if it is kept in perfect condition, reduces its value. I was convinced, though, that Jacob was worth it, and I allowed him to fly the planes as much as possible so he could get his hours. Naturally, I tried to work in scouting missions, baggage hauls, etc., to mitigate the expense. Jacob was both a huge risk and investment for me. He could cost me a fortune and then never become my pilot.

It became a game. Jacob would return from a flight, check the Hobbs meter (much like a mileage meter on a car, except that instead of miles, it logs hours that the plane has flown) and then get into that aggravatingly familiar seated position and carefully enter his hours into the log book.

I was thinking, *This is Jacob's future. He is living his dream and I am proud to be a part of that.* Soon he would be a full-fledged Alaskan bush pilot. I cannot stress enough how hard and expensive it is for a non-resident of Alaska to qualify, and Jacob was a non-resident. On top of that I paid him well for the hours he put in as my employee and would pay him pilot's wages when he flew for me plus other benefits. In other words, I would not get a financial return on Jacob. I could hire other pilots that were already licensed, but I didn't care, because that is how much I cared about Jacob.

I spent hours with Jacob going over various possible landing sites on the hillsides and asking him, "Would you land here?" Often I was testing him. If he responded incorrectly, I would jump all over him and tell him if he ever landed there, I would "pull his ticket." Then I would explain why that was a bad choice, maybe even life threatening. I taught him about bog, where the land looks nice and smooth but is soft and mushy and will grab the wheels of your plane and overturn you in a heartbeat.

I would walk off the terrain of possible landing sites with him and point out the things to look for, and we would measure it together and then fly over it to get the perspective from the air. Believe me; things look much different from the air. Good veteran bush pilots will come in low and slow and actually stall the plane very close to the ground at 45 to 50 knots, then lightly drag their wheels to test the surface. Talk about guts and a steady touch! Frozen humps look good from the air but are deadly. I showed Jacob how to look for small rocks, gravel-like in appearance. This is usually an indicator of a good surface. However, a bush pilot must be wary of any indentations in the ground. A wheel can dip and flip the plane before you can spell ptarmigan.

Once a safe landing is made, especially on a new slope, the pilot must check out the terrain thoroughly. When they are satisfied it is a safe spot and have walked it off to measure it, they will mark the location into their GPS. Jacob was shown how critical it was to find two or three ways to enter and exit a landing site, if possible, due to shifting winds, fog or any other conditions that may arise.

I have barely scratched the surface of things that must be learned by a good bush pilot. The other pilots and I taught Jacob a ton of stuff he needed to learn. Through it all, he was a sponge and continued to impress everyone with his ability to retain the information and with his natural instincts for flying. I invested in Jacob and his flying because I felt his great desire and passion. I also wanted him to fly for me, but deeper than that, I took pride in seeing him progress. I guess in a way he affected me like the son I never had, and my love for him continued to flourish.

At first, he flew from our airport landing strip and back. He progressed from that to landing on homemade strips and wide gravel bars on streams and lakes. Gravel bars on riverbanks offer their own challenges. Many are very nice with good, firm sand but still can be tricky. The true test is when you move from the gravel bars to the ridges on the hillsides.

Some remote landing sites are so prime and safe, and landed on so often, that everyone uses them and they become a "community" site, primarily used as a staging area. Planes a step up in size can land on them, thus bringing in larger loads and more passengers. From there the smaller bush planes are used to ferry people and supplies. One such site near us is called Navajo Strip. After Jacob proved himself on the sand bars, he landed at the Navajo Strip and then began landing on hillside ridges. He progressed through these stages almost without a hiccup.

I don't think one can truly understand Alaska without a good understanding of the bush pilots, dog mushers and river-runners who have braved the elements to explore this amazing state. "Sno-gos" (snowmobiles) have expanded man's range in flatter areas and on frozen rivers and lakes, but the bush plane is at the core of traveling in the wilderness. As the horse is to the cowboy and the dog is to the musher, so the plane is to the guide. Nothing has replaced the bush plane, and I can't imagine they will be replaced in the

foreseeable future. There is a complex network of pilots. Most remote villages rely on them for mail, supplies, travel and emergencies.

Cessna Aircraft Company and Piper Aircraft have made some of the most famous and popular bush planes in Alaska. In order to describe to you the planes most often used by bush pilots, the following comparisons may help. The PA-18 (Piper Aircraft) Cub is a Jeep Willys, the Cessna 185 is a Ferrari and the Cessna 206 is the Alaskan SUV Cadillac. The Cub and Cessna have a wheel under the tail. They are affectionately referred to as "taildraggers." The Cub holds two, a pilot and one passenger, and the 185 carries five, yet a good bush pilot can land the 185 on some of the better hillside ridges. The 206 has a nose wheel and holds six passengers. Larger planes that can land on decent homemade strips include the Cessna Caravan, the new Kodiak Quest and DeHavilland Beaver.

Overall, a tail wheeler/dragger is probably safer than the planes with a nose wheel. (A tail wheeler has one small tire in back, two regular sized in front; and the other planes have two in back and one in front.) If the nose wheel collapses, you are in serious trouble when you land because the nose of the plane, which is where the pilot and prop are, will dive forward into the ground with terrific force. Whereas on a tail-dragger, if the tail wheel fails, a pilot can "pancake" and slide around in more of a stalled crash with the bottom rear of the plane receiving most of the damage.

The planes I have mentioned handle the majority of the Alaskan wilderness flying chores. I own a P-18 Super Cub, a Cessna 185 and a 206. It takes all three in good condition to handle the hunting and fishing trips. The Cub is the one used for those tricky landings on small ridges. Often the experience of being flown into the bush in these planes is the highlight of the trip for the guests. Even after many years and thousands of trips myself, I still revel in the experience.

Guides and pilots have some longstanding, unspoken rules and policies. When you are in remote areas, these customs are not something to scoff at. A breach of these understandings is handled forcefully and immediately, occasionally with gunplay, I have been told. On the hundreds of miles of ridges and canyons that we hunt, you wouldn't think that there would be much conflict, but the places on which safe landings can be made are not plentiful.

No one privately owns the land, but if you have located a sweet little prime hunting spot, and you found and developed a nearby landing strip to access it, you try to keep it a secret. Sure, tents are hard to hide and secrets like that don't last long; however, if you hunt there consistently year after year, you come to think of it as *your* hunting grounds. As a courtesy, most guides will not land there during the times you usually use it.

However, there is no law that says a remote landing place is exclusive. It is, after all, public land. It is sorta like that parking place in front of your house. You don't own it, but most neighborly folks will not infringe. Sometimes, though, without realizing it I have set up on a site not knowing that another guide had "claimed" it. I advised Jacob about all of this as part of his bush plane education.

Recently I set up a tent in such a place. I had previously flown over and spotted some nice big game animals nearby. What I expressly did not see was anyone else in the area. I had flown in tents and gear and was going about getting the camp ready for incoming clients. While doing this and minding my business, I heard some shouting. I looked up and stomping quickly toward me, red-faced and carrying a menacing looking rifle in the ready position, was another guide.

He was yelling, "I have hunted this site for 20 years. You have no right to be here. This is my ridge and this is my property!" I looked at him, then at his gun, and considered the options. I could argue with him and tell him to get lost because I had gotten there first and I had hunted there previously myself. I had as much claim to it as he did. It was most definitely not his property.

What I have learned is this: Lazy or inefficient guides will locate a few good spots that don't involve much time, trouble or expense for them to get their clients to, and they will wear these sites out. They will run everyone else off. Good guides don't rely on just a couple of locations. They keep in reserve many areas they can fly to and hunt. Doing this takes a lot of diligence and patient scouting to locate and test landing strips to make sure they are safe. Once located, the site is logged into their GPS. A prudent guide keeps up with what the animals are actually doing each year, even though this may take many costly hours of flying and scouting. These sites are never divulged to anyone but your pilot, whom you hope you can trust. He knows he will be out of a job immediately if he betrays your confidence.

Animals don't necessarily frequent the same ridges or localities each year, although they do favor certain ones, and this is even truer for those areas that guides saturate by repeatedly bringing in hunters to the same spot. Little do the hunters know that many prior groups, week after week and year after year, may have already camped there, or that several other groups may even have been placed close by at the same time they are camped. No matter what their guide has glowingly said, these clients have little chance of success.

Well, the other guide continued ranting, dropping in a few choice swear words and waving his rifle ominously. "I want you off this ridge pronto. I don't know who you think you are, but you and everyone here better get off my ridge!" As he said this, he waved his weapon in the direction of the tent I had set up. By now, he had moved to within a few yards, whereupon he stopped and began glaring at me over the barrel of his gun. He did seem a mite taken aback because I was so calm and had not reacted. He certainly realized he wasn't intimidating me in the least.

I looked at him, wanting to shove his rifle into places that the sun doesn't shine. I knew that if I left, I would have to re-call the plane, break camp, re-route the clients and then hastily set up somewhere else, hopefully before dark. Yet in spite of this, I also try to maintain goodwill overall with the guides in the area. Sort of like the prison code. Show respect; get respect, regardless of the issue. Moreover, if your plane crashes, those other guides may be the only ones close enough to help. I also knew it wasn't just about me. I didn't want to put the clients in danger.

I shrugged and said levelly, "I suggest you put that pea-shooter away because you just might hurt yourself. If you don't, I'll wrap it around your neck." He looked startled at my calm but flinty response and started to reply, but before he could say something stupid, I interjected, "Nobody here knew anything about this being your 'spot,' mister; however, I'll give you the benefit of the doubt and find another place, so keep a lid on it." He muttered something, but I turned around and ignored him. I was mad, and honestly, I never have reacted kindly to playground bullies.

Every guide out there will tell you about similar run-ins. I am sure there have been people killed over our wilderness version of "claim jumping." I have had other guides jump my spots and even steal the GPS locations from my plane. Trying to find a way to cope with this, the Fish and Game has instituted a rule that a guide can't bother another hunter by landing or setting up camp too close to someone else's site, assuming that the other site is already in place. I suspect the interpretation of "too close" is open to debate, but I would estimate that you would want to be over a mile away at the minimum, and usually farther.

In response to this law, some disreputable guides will fly in even before hunting season starts and set up fake camps. Such a camp may remain empty for many weeks, but the guide can claim that someone is encroaching if he sees another camp being set up in the area. Yes, there is also a rule about being in one spot for an extended period, but in the vast wilderness, there are no parking checkers to mark your tires and cite you for overstaying your allotted time.

Some guides simply don't care and don't follow the rules, spoken or otherwise. They don't usually last long, but they are a pain, nevertheless. However, they will hastily come if your plane crashes—that is, once you have been airlifted out. They swoop in and steal parts off your plane.

Plane parts are expensive. Custom balloon tires with rims and brakes are several thousand per. I have had stuff stolen from downed planes more than once. Usually everyone is aware of what's up, so it is wise not to make too many enemies in this business. How does that saying go? Keep your friends close and your enemies even closer.

Well, Jacob was a quick study and learned about the nuances of flying, about the rules of the bush and much more. He would listen carefully to stories like this and file them away in his mind. The more he learned, the more he loved it, and he knew flying was going to be his life. I just hoped bush flying wasn't going to end it. I have lost more than one close friend or guide through plane crashes, so I probably went overboard in trying to teach Jacob. This was his heart, so he listened intently and asked many great questions.

Feeling His Oats

Time passed, it was Jacob's second or third year and he had continued to receive compliments on his flying. He was a natural and everyone was impressed with him. Not one time had he ever damaged a plane or had an accident, even as a green pilot. He was good and in time would be great. I was happy to have him. However, there is that moment when the student begins to feel he is equal to his teachers or knows something his teachers don't. This is a dangerous time.

Jacob had occasionally questioned me about some of the areas where I told him not to land. In particular, he always felt that he could land on the valley floor in some of the huge marshy areas. He felt that the Super Cub equipped with large custom balloon tires, specifically designed to distribute weight and lessen impact, could handle this terrain. He was not fully convinced that the weight of the plane would be a problem on these admittedly soft spots.

In addition, he and Jon, our fabulous cook, loved to go out hunting for "sheds" (discarded animal horns). In fact, it was an obsession. They would see a set from the air and risk their lives, my plane, their and the lodge's reputation to get them. Many don't realize this, but *intact* sheds with skulls are in the record books right alongside regular kills.

Finding sheds becomes a passion for many of the assistant guides. Some of these racks have been shed naturally in spring (bull moose shed their horns around March), or the animals have been killed by predators, or have died by other means, leaving the horns intact. We use them in various ways and often mark remote runways with sheds. Caribou horns are especially good for this purpose because they stand up tall. We will tie a flag, ribbon or piece of cloth to them, thus creating a homemade flag to show how the wind is blowing. There are sheds all over the lodge.

It is fun to find beautiful racks. In many places, sheds are collected and sold as is or carved skillfully in various ways. For those who don't want to shoot an animal, this is actually a great way to "hunt" and obtain a rack without the extra work, expense or harm. They are listed in the record books, the same as a kill, without a shot being fired.

I was told that a caribou intact skull and shed at one time was listed as the top trophy rack ever gotten, or close to it. So, it can become addicting. I have given away beautiful sheds created by grizzly kills where part of the skull/head and fur was still attached and mounts depicting the epic struggle beautifully made.

Over time, Jon and Jacob became fast friends and more and more enamored with collecting sheds. They would often fly on scouting missions looking for them. They would push the limits of their plane and their ability to get at them. One time Jacob and I were flying through a valley and saw a recent grizzly bear kill, evidenced by a huge moose shed sticking out of a mound. Jacob immediately wanted to go after it.

A mound is often created when a grizzly makes a kill. The bear will pile up grass, dirt, rocks and whatever else is close by in order to hide its kill. It will do this by using its front paws like a backhoe to cover the meat. Grizzlies are incredible diggers. Often the mound over the meat is three or four feet high. The bear will  return later and feast. Bears enjoy the meat more when it has decayed and softened. Seems the more stinky and rotten it is, the more they love it. I have staked out many a mound or decayed carcass to get a bear.

In this case, the horns were still visible at the top of the mound, and I had no doubt that the grizzly likely guarding it was not about to let anyone near its kill. Jacob wanted the horns badly. He said to me, "I can land in that meadow over there and we can get those horns." I was startled at this. I said, "Jacob, don't you remember the things we taught you? You can never land in a meadow like that. Don't ever risk a plane doing something that foolish. That is a horrible idea and it could cost you your life, not to mention the loss of my plane. Trust me, if you do that to me I will fire you on the spot!"

I went on to explain to him that a meadow (low marshy area between two ridges) looks inviting and safe from the air, but underneath it is bog and mud. From the air, a meadow looks perfect for landing. Many green pilots make that mistake. Because it is so low it collects water, yet this water remains invisible since it is covered by muskeg and tundra, and consequently, it becomes soft and soggy.

In places, merely stepping in it will cause you to sink up to your hips. The moist "skin of a meadow" will not hold a 2,000-pound plane. Moose love these spots since they contain tender, fresh shoots, and the larger predators don't have an advantage because their bulk and weight and the soggy surface make it awkward for them to corner their prey.

I pointed out to Jacob a ridge about three miles away. It was a ridge with which I was familiar. I told him that if he was that desperate to get those horns, he could land there, hike down and hike back. It would be a six-mile round-trip, but if the horns were that special, then it might be worth it. Jacob just kept quiet, but I could tell he wanted those horns. However, I was sure the admonition to him had been sufficient, and as we flew off, I turned my mind to more pressing matters.

On a couple of other occasions, we again flew over the place where the horns were, and Jacob would look long-ingly out of the plane window at them. He would say, "Rock, I can land there, I can do it." I told him. "Jacob, I know this valley like the back of my hand, and I will give you the back of my hand if you ever try to land there. That meadow is marshy and it won't support this plane. If you want those horns so bad, land on that ridge I told you about and do some hiking and packing. Otherwise, don't try it. I know that meadow looks like a beautiful Kansas grain field, but it is more like a Venus Fly Trap. It will swallow you up in a heartbeat!"

Jacob nodded and said, "Okay, Rock, you're the boss." After that, the moose shed wasn't brought up again.

A few days later, we were ferrying some clients and equipment out to our remote lodge on the Holitna River from Lake Clark. We loaded up the plane Jacob was to fly (the Cub) and sent him on his way early in the morning. Another pilot and I planned to follow several hours later in a larger plane, bringing the clients.

Jacob tends to be pretty quiet, but this morning he seemed more cheerful and energetic than usual and even appeared to be in a hurry. I was busy and didn't notice, but later it would all make sense to me. Jacob quickly helped load the Cub, and then with a cheery wave, he was off. He was supposed to fly to the Holitna and drop off the supplies on a simple runway-to-runway flight.

A few hours later, Joel's wife, Lisa, who lives at Lake Clark, received a call that "Jacob was down." She relayed this immediately to Joel and he informed everyone right away. This sent a chill through all of us. Jacob had flown off alone over remote, wild terrain on a 280-mile round-trip in a plane loaded with baggage, and somewhere along the way he had crashed. I was scared to death. I notified the proper authorities and relayed the information to dozens of local pilots, who promptly launched their aircrafts in desperate search of Jacob.

The reason Lisa had gotten the call was that Alaska's Rescue Coordination Center (RCC), had gotten word via a jet airliner at 41,000 feet that a Super Cub 905 was "down, in distress, possible fire." The term "possible fire" was used because Jacob's distress call was weak and the jet pilot wasn't sure what he had heard. The contact number Jacob gave the pilot was Joel's home phone.

The jet pilot had radioed Anchorage International Airport and given them the information, and they called Joel. Since Joel wasn't at home, Lisa answered. The only information we received was that "Jacob was down and needed help." That could mean anything, and we feared the worst. More horrifying yet, we had no clue where Jacob had crashed.

SAR (Search and Rescue) immediately launched. Joel and I prayed, then rushed to Joel's plane and flew off to do our own search. I just kept praying that Jacob wasn't dead. Somehow, I felt responsible, and I was distraught that this young man might lose his life. Joel and I brainstormed and decided Jacob might have hit the mountains while paralleling the intended route, possibly due to a downdraft, and if so, his chances of survival were slim.

The flight plan Jacob logged was simple. It listed the planned route as being from Lake Clark airfield to the Holitna Lodge, which has its own airstrip. As a bird flies, it is 138 miles. Consequently, this was the route and direction everyone flew in search of Jacob. Joel and I flew back and forth across this route in a lazy "S" fashion covering many miles along mountain ridges and rivers, then back out over the valleys. We flew several hours in this manner, looking frantically for any sign of Jacob or the plane, and saw nothing. In time, getting low on gas and lower in spirits, we arrived at the Holitna, sweating, dismayed and praying but with no idea where Jacob was. No one else had seen him either.

However, when we landed on the airstrip at the Holitna Lodge, Joel and I were immediately struck by what we saw. Neither Jacob nor the plane was there, but it was obvious that Jacob had been there. The baggage and equipment given him had been unloaded, which was proof he had arrived. The puzzling thing was that the gear had obviously been unloaded in great haste. This was evidenced by what we observed as soon as we touched down on the landing strip.

Joel taxied his plane to a stop, and we got out and looked at the stuff we had put into the plane for Jacob to transport. It was unloaded too close to the runway and was in great disarray. After standing there and looking at it for a moment, the truth hit me. Jacob had quickly gotten the supplies off the Cub, setting them down close to the airstrip, and in his haste to leave had "propped" them (hit them with air from the propeller) during his quick maneuver in turning the plane around. He had powered the plane around by using his flaps and accelerating the propeller hard to turn the plane, instead of moving the plane around manually.

Once the powerful blast of air hit the baggage and equipment, it had blown and scattered them like rustling leaves in the wind. Fishing poles, life jackets, lunches, suitcases, clothing, etc., were spread all over the ground. The question was, Why? Why had Jacob been in such a hurry? This was not like him. Joel stared at the mess and was stumped. He couldn't come up with an answer. After awhile he shook his head in exasperation and went into the lodge to get some food. I just stood there staring at the debris, a little idea worming its way into my head.

I felt like I was in one of those "profiler" shows where the investigator is at a crime scene, then pauses and tries to picture in his mind's eye what happened. I did that, picturing Jacob in my thoughts, seeing him quickly taking stuff off the plane and rapidly unloading. I flashed back to the happy mood he was in when he left Lake Clark and how he was in a hurry even then. That suggested to me that his urgency was not due to something that had happened en route to the Holitna. Something was pressing him *before* he left. What could it have been?

I continued to stare at the scene around me. I stood in almost a trance, eyes closed, seeing Jacob and trying to read his mind via the flashing images whirling through my head. Like a flash, a voice popped into my head. Jacob's voice. "I can land there, Rocky, I know I can." Instantly, I knew where Jacob had gone. He had flown to where we had seen that moose shed. He was determined to prove me wrong. He was determined to land in that treacherous meadow!

I quickly compared my conclusion with the evidence. Jacob had left Lake Clark in a hurry. Assuming I was right, then Jacob knew that if he flew like the wind and could get the stuff he carried unloaded without delay, he might have time to alter his predetermined course, head off-route to the site of the moose shed on the grizzly mound, land, grab it, take off and head for Lake Clark. If successful, no one would be the wiser. He had little time to spare for the mission I was now convinced he had set out to do. It all fit. I knew in my heart he had crashed in that meadow.

That meadow is between Holitna and Lake Clark, but it is quite a ways off line. No one searching for Jacob would have flown that much off the course of his stated flight plan looking for him.

Joel had returned from the lodge and was aimlessly wandering amidst the scattered gear in complete consternation. I swiftly turned to him and yelled, "I know where he is, Joel! I know where he is!"

Joel looked at me in complete disbelief. How could this stuff lying in total disarray reveal to me where Jacob was? He hollered back at me, "Where is he, Rocky?" I was already rushing to his plane, wanting to refuel it quickly from my storage tank. I screamed back, "I'll tell you when we get in the air. Just help me get this plane gassed up so we can get out of here fast!" Joel didn't have to be asked twice. He knew I had an uncanny knack of solving wilderness puzzles. Soon we were off and flying.

Once safely airborne, he spoke to me through the headphones in the plane. "Okay, Rock, where are we headed?"

Rite of Passage

We have named most of the locations we frequent, and after awhile, it is just a matter of saying to the pilot, "Take me to Rifle Ridge" or "Take me to the Navajo Strip." Otherwise, we use GPS coordinates. I said to Joel, "Take me to Grizzly Gorge." He glanced quickly at me and then got back to the business of flying. When he responded, I could hear the puzzlement in his voice, "Why are we going there, Rocky?" I carefully explained to him my suspicions about where Jacob had gone and why he had been in such a hurry.

After I finished, Joel immediately protested. He wasn't buying it. He said, "I'm sorry, Rock, but you got it wrong this time. Jacob would never do such a stupid thing as that." I didn't respond. Whether I was right or wrong would be confirmed soon. I just fervently hoped first that Jacob was okay, and second that the plane wasn't in too bad of shape. At least I had some hope. If he had crashed in the meadow, his chances of survival were much greater than if he had crashed on a rocky mountainside.

Joel kept quiet and I could tell he was in deep thought. Despite making a beeline to the site to which I had directed him, we still kept searching the landscape for Jacob. No sense in wasting this flight. If Jacob was not there, we wanted to know which areas we had covered so that we would not duplicate our efforts in our continuing search to find him.

Upon arrival at the location of the moose shed, Joel slowed his plane down considerably and made a slow pass over the site. At first we didn't see anything, and Joel circled and began crisscrossing over the valley where the horns were. I could sense that he was relieved that we had not seen Jacob and that his first instincts seemed right. Naturally, he did not want me to be right because of what it would suggest about Jacob. He had grown very fond of Jacob, as we all had, and Joel had great faith in Jacob.

Now, recall that we were in Joel's plane, not mine. Then, over the airplane radio, we heard a soft voice, Jacob's voice, shocking us both, and especially Joel. "Joel, is that you?" Jacob asked. Joel was stunned yet also relieved to hear Jacob's voice and that we had found him. Joel asked, "Jacob, you okay?" Jacob replied, "Yeah, I'm okay, Joel. Can you help me?" What a relief for both of us. It was really Jacob's voice! He was alive. He was okay! The emotions that swept through us were immense. For a few moments as we circled trying to spot Jacob and the downed plane, the air inside our cockpit was pulsating with joy.

Those feelings didn't last long, however. Soon we saw the plane. It was buried nose first in the marsh. Jacob was a few yards away, sitting disconsolately under some small spruce trees. As the realization of what Jacob had tried to do sunk in, I thought Joel was going to blow a main gasket. I can't recall seeing him so angry in all the time I have known him.

It also occurred to us that Jacob was unaware that I was in the plane with Joel. I suspect that Jacob had told the pilot in the jet to contact Joel, specifically, hoping Joel would discreetly help him get out of this mess. Whatever the reason, it would not have mattered, because plane incidents and accidents cannot be hidden. The FAA requires extensive reporting, and damaged planes must be rebuilt to rigid standards before new certifications can be issued.

We circled a few more times, made sure Jacob was okay and then radioed for Jeremy, who flies a Cub similar to mine, to come in and pick him up. We were in a 206, which was too large to land on the ridge nearby. We gave Jeremy coordinates to the ridge. Once we were sure that Jacob was able to walk without further injury, we instructed him to walk to the ridge to meet Jeremy. We called off the search and notified SAR, and everyone involved was thrilled to hear that Jacob was alive and not seriously injured. His pride and the plane had suffered huge blows, however.

On the flight back to Lake Clark, Joel got madder and madder. He was so furious that Jacob had betrayed the bush pilot profession, betrayed him and me. He kept ranting, "I can't believe he did that! Didn't he listen to anything Jeremy and I told him? Does he think he is bulletproof? What was he thinking? I am done with him. I will never work with him again. He put other pilots in danger who were trying desperately to locate him, flying low into canyons and other dangerous areas with swirling, unpredictable winds, just to try to find him. And for what? A stupid shed! And he calls me to bail him out! I know the plane crash didn't kill him, but when I get my hands on him, I will!"

I kept silent during most of this tirade, but I was in full concurrence. Jacob had risked his life and much more on a useless moose shed. Others had risked their lives and spent costly flying and man-hours looking for him. I knew the repairs on the plane alone would cost me thousands of dollars, money not covered by insurance. I was sickened that our prized up-and-coming pilot, in whom I had placed so much faith and invested time, money and myself, and who had so deeply touched my heart, had betrayed himself and me.

We were stunned, not only because Jacob was a good pilot and knew better, but because he had made such an impact on all of us, demonstrating both character and trustworthiness. Yet in this case, he had let his obsession and desire for a set of moose shed horns cloud his thinking. He had risked his future, my livelihood, his life, the reputation of those who had trained him, the plane and the lives of other pilots for nothing.

Joel and I felt as though we had been on a roller coaster; we were two emotional wrecks. We had experienced tremendous stress and fear for several hours while looking for Jacob and the fear kept increasing the longer the search went on without success. Once we ran out of options and knew of nowhere else to look, we began to feel helpless.

When I got the inspiration of where he might be, while standing on the runway at the Holitna, it had been like a last ditch effort. If he had not been there, where else could we search? Normally, no one would have searched that area because it wasn't close to Jacob's flight plan, and this is a vast wilderness. Then, when we had found him alive and well, we had experienced immense relief and joy, which had been quickly dispelled by our deep anger and disappointment at the foolish decision Jacob had made.

Jeremy flew to the ridge and picked up a sad and shaken Jacob, who had wisely left the moose shed for the grizzly. Jeremy has had his share of heartache in the wilderness, and he was very good with Jacob, trying hard to reassure him. They talked a lot on the way back to the lodge. Jacob was very subdued, however, and some of the cockiness that all good pilots possess—and, in fact, need to possess to some degree—was gone.

Joel and I were sitting on a couch in the middle of the lodge when Jacob arrived. Joel wanted to fire Jacob. He was so disappointed, and he just couldn't believe what had happened. Our anger had not subsided much. That Cub had been my baby lamb, and I cherished it. Cubs are no longer built, so they are sacred in Alaska. I had spent time and money transforming mine from a workhorse to a show horse.

It was a Super Cub with all the bells and whistles. It was also my livelihood and lifeline to the bush. Now the plane was doubtful for the upcoming hunting season. Not only would I have to bear the expense of salvage, rebuilding the plane and recertification, I would have to pay a lot more to use other pilots and their planes to fulfill the obligations to the hunters. Once again, I was hit with a huge financial blow of tens of thousands of dollars, money I didn't have to spare.

I was dismally calculating all of this in my mind when Jeremy and Jacob arrived at the entrance to the lodge. They opened the door and stood in the doorway. Jeremy looked up almost at once and spotted Joel and me. We just sat there saying nothing and not offering any greeting. Jeremy started walking over to where we were sitting, but Jacob did not follow, opting instead to wait at the entrance, obviously not wanting to confront me just yet. Jeremy stopped, engaged in some small chat with us and then, instinctively sensing impending doom, deftly disappeared. Honestly, I was so upset; I don't even remember a word Jeremy said. Probably something about "taking it easy on the kid," but believe me, neither Joel nor I were in a forgiving mood.

After Jeremy left, I looked at Jacob. He knew he could not avoid it any longer. He dropped his head a little, shuffled up to us and then stood meekly in front of Joel and me, sort of like a whipped puppy. We initially looked him over to determine if he was physically okay, although we knew he had hiked out of difficult terrain with no problem, and the early reports from Jeremy had been encouraging, if not conclusive. I noticed that Jacob's clothes were disheveled, his hair had grass fragments in it and his face and neck were sweaty and dirty, but overall he seemed to be breathing without discomfort and wasn't exhibiting any physical pain. It was easy to tell that his pain was mostly coming from his heart.

I will give him this. There is an old saw about good negotiators and that the best ones never speak first. That concept applied here. The first person to speak loses. Jacob kept quiet. I waited a few moments and tried to control the anger welling up inside of me. I wanted to get up and shake Jacob so hard that the foolishness in him would fall out and leave for good. I then fervently wished he could come up with a plausible explanation for why he had disobeyed strict orders and explain to me what the heck he thought he was doing. Jacob shifted uneasily and then raised his eyes to mine and met my gaze straight on.

I began in a firm and controlled voice, "Just what do you want me to say to your parents, Jacob? Just exactly what do I tell them? Sorry, folks, your son crashed and almost died trying to get moose horn sheds!" I paused and continued, "Well, Jacob, you can pack your bags and you can go home. You're done." I stopped a moment for full effect, and then I said very forcefully, "Or you can stay and face this like a man, suffer the consequences and work it out!"

Jacob was startled at this, almost as if I had hit him. My meaning was obvious. I would offer him another chance, but it was going to cost him work, time, effort and a commitment to prove to us that he was the man we originally thought he was. He would have to convince us that something like this would never happen again. His reputation and our trust in him had been shattered. It would be up to him to decide if he wanted to take on the daunting task of rebuilding it.

I am not sure why I decided at that moment to give him another chance. Maybe because I loved him and did not want it to end this way. It would not be easy for him, I knew. This was a harsh climate. If he chose to stay, he could not hide nor pretend it didn't happen. This was serious. An unnecessarily risky pilot is despised in Alaska. He would have to take responsibility and face his and our friends and all of the other guides and pilots. He would have to find a way to show them he deserved another chance. I left the decision up to him. I had offered him his rite of passage.

After I finished, Joel stared hard at Jacob and began to address him, beginning much the same way I did. "That's right, Jacob. What the blazes do we tell your parents? That you were killed trying to get a moose shed? Is that a good reason to die? You should be done. That would be my vote. I don't have a clue why Rocky is giving you another chance."

Now, Joel is an outstanding pilot and never takes an inappropriate risk. Franklin Graham, who has flown and been flown worldwide, once told me that in his opinion, Joel Natwick was the best all-around pilot he had ever met. Joel can fly anything with wings, including Super Cubs, cargo planes, private jets and even helicopters. If he could find a way to strap himself to a penguin, I bet he could fly that. He is also an outstanding airplane mechanic and has attended every significant school there is. He may not get some of the recognition that others do because he rarely shows off or takes chances, but the guy can flat out fly planes.

I consider Joel one of the foremost pilots I have ever met, so when he speaks, I listen. Jacob was listening to him now, intently. As I watched Joel rip Jacob apart, I discovered that this normally mild-mannered man had missed one of his callings—as a trash talking drill sergeant in the U.S. Marines. He skinned Jacob like a punk soldier who had gone AWOL. I won't go into all the specifics of that complete dressing down, but suffice it to say, Joel scolded, scalded, shredded and stripped Jacob down to skin and bones.

Whew! I was sitting right next to Joel, nodding my head up and down in hearty agreement with each thrust. I don't think I have ever seen him so passionate. Why? It was obvious. Joel loved Jacob too.

He finished, "Next time it will be your life, Jacob. Look at all the lives you risked that went in search for you, pushing the limits of their fuel and ability to find you.

And for what? A dead shed. That's what! If something like this ever comes close to happening again, I am finished with you, young man, for good! Are you trying to destroy Rocky's livelihood?"

Joel was right. Pilots are paid high wages, yet when they crash, even if totally their fault, never offer of feel obligated to help pay for the very expensive uninsured repairs of the plane or costs to extract them, yet they still want their pay.

Jacob stood there, eyes glistening, pursing his lips and blinking rapidly. He did not respond. When Joel had finished, I took a deep breath and said, "Well, okay, Jacob, now it is up to you. You can tuck your tail between your legs and get your butt outta here on the next flight, or you can face it like a man. The choice, young man, is up to you!"

Once I finished it got really quiet, and we just waited for a reaction. Nothing else was said. Joel and I kept looking at Jacob, waiting for him to respond. He stood there for a few more moments, looking at us both, and said nothing. Then he turned and trudged slowly out of the lodge and went to his cabin. Joel and I looked at each other. We both knew in our guts that Jacob was not going to stay and stick it out. Jacob was done. I felt a deep sadness envelop me.

Jacob did not show up for dinner that night, and the crew was quiet and somber. Our clients had been kept in the dark about the incident. We'd fished them at another location and carried on as usual during the day with alternate guides and boats. They were busy chatting about their day, but among the staff, the mood was very gloomy. All of us loved Jacob and believed he would be gone come sunup.

Sharon and I discussed it that night. She had been so thrilled, as we all were, that Jacob was okay, but she was almost as upset as Joel and I about the stupid decision Jacob had made and the loss of our plane. Hunting season was typically the most lucrative part of our year. Now, just before hunting season was to open, our plane was down. Sharon also was deeply saddened that Jacob was sure to be leaving. In his quiet way, Jacob had reached the hearts of many.

I knew that night would be tough on him. He had been curried, feted and ballyhooed for the entire time he had been working for me. Everyone had continually marveled and told him how good he was. He was a natural born pilot, a young man with a lot of character, and he had been living his dream. Now, in one gruesome day, he had to face himself. He had to choose whether he was going to stick it out and face the music or fade away ingloriously. I had a lot of faith in Jacob, but the meek way he had turned and left, without a response or explanation to us, had led me to believe he would no longer be flying my planes. I was sure he would be seeking a new path and that he would be going home.

I had seen Jacob's confidence waver, and the irony was not lost on me. Overconfidence in a pilot can be his greatest enemy, but under-confidence is just as deadly. There has to be a fine line, a perfect balance in your faith in your abilities, combined with your wisdom in decision-making and knowing your limits. I knew Jacob would have a tough time finding that balance in his life as a bush pilot again, especially if he quit now.

Strangely, in spite of it all, I still believed in him. If Jacob could control his desire to make the plane do things it wasn't meant to do and stick within the fundamental parameters for himself and his craft, he would become an awesome bush pilot. However, as I drifted off to sleep, I did not have much hope that I would ever see Jacob fly again. I eventually dozed off to a very fitful sleep.

The next morning Joel came over early for cinnamon rolls. He'd had a rough night too. His first comment to me was, "This guy is probably worth working with, Rock." I knew he meant Jacob.

Obviously, Joel had worked it out with himself last night once he was alone with his thoughts. He had calmed down and changed his mind. He had come to the same conclusion that I had, namely that Jacob was worth saving. He said to me, "If Jacob can buck up and make it through this, he will become a great pilot. Our actions yesterday with him will save his life someday, or someone else's, because he will have learned his lesson permanently."

Everyone showed up for breakfast—everyone except Jacob. We were all sitting at the table eating listlessly, and again, the tone was quiet. All at once all conversation stopped and heads turned toward the entrance. There, framed in the doorway, stood Jacob. He looked tired and shaken, but resolute. He walked straight over to the table near where I was sitting and no one spoke. He looked directly at me and said, "Can we go somewhere and talk for a minute?" I said, "Sure," expecting that Jacob was saying goodbye, had his bags packed and wanted to finalize preparations to leave.

I got up, leaving my partially eaten meal. When I did, so did Sharon. She, Jacob and I walked to a private room nearby. Not a word was spoken by anyone inside the lodge, and as we walked, our shoes echoing eerily on the floor, I felt as though we were marching a prisoner to his last meal. The people at the table just stared after us. I noticed that Jacob's clothes looked as if he had slept in them. I could tell he'd had a long night. Upon reaching the room, I walked in and sat down on a couch, Sharon by my side, leaving the door partially open. Jacob remained standing between the door and us, facing us squarely.

After everyone got still I said, "Okay, Jacob, what do you have to say for yourself?" He stood there fidgeting nervously and then, very softly, began speaking, struggling to get the words out. I leaned forward to better hear him and felt a surge within me when he said, "I'm going to stick it out, Rocky." I was shocked because I had expected to hear quite the opposite, but I was secretly happy when the full meaning of those words dawned on me. I could tell that Jacob was truly remorseful.

I noticed that Joel was at the door and he had heard Jacob too. He walked over to Jacob, put his arm around him and said, "These types of things will make you a better pilot if you truly learn from them." I was strangely fascinated at how Joel could manage his cinnamon roll in one hand, hot coffee in the other and still be comforting Jacob. He then turned to me and began affirming Jacob. He said, "Rock, this guy is worth working with. I know he will make the right decisions for you in the future." I could tell that these reassuring words meant a lot to Jacob. He set his teeth, tried to smile and looked at me.

I said to him, "It will be a long road back, son. From now on, you are only a fishing guide. You will take clients fishing, clean fish, clean boats, pack gear and earn our trust every step of the way." Jacob said, "Okay," and turned to leave. He is certainly a man of few words.

As he started to walk away I said, "Always remember this, Jacob: A great pilot has exactly the same number of safe landings as he does take-offs." Jacob nodded in agreement and went back to his cabin.

After Jacob left, Joel looked at me and said, "I think you handled this with a lot of wisdom. It's the right decision to give him another chance. What we did brought the truth home to him, and this will teach him to be a real pilot. I think he grasps now how much a plane crash can affect our lives, how deadly they can be and how even financially they are devastating. He knows now how easy it is to make a wrong choice and hurt a lot of people. I foresee that he will become the bush pilot that all of us will be proud of. This day will save his and others' lives down the road."

I looked at Joel and said, "I totally agree." I thought , *This young man will become my future pilot. He just stepped up to the plate and showed real character by facing the music and wanting to make things right.* Little did I know then the impact Jacob's decision would have later on his life, my life and the lives of my family.

Jacob had come to his defining moment. He had faced his demons. He had been presented his rite of passage and he had chosen the journey of manhood.

His mom remarked to me later, "As you know, Rocky, Jacob is quiet and reserved and unsure of himself around people sometimes. When he gets back from his summers in Alaska, though, we cannot believe how his confidence continues to grow. For the first couple of days we can't shut him up! He just talks and talks."

Jacob, talking and talking? Now that I gotta see. Anyway, after that it was as if someone had unlocked his cage and set him free. His experiences in Alaska have truly brought a real maturity to his heart and life. Jacob came to Alaska as a boy, but he is well on his way to being a real man.

Chapter Eight

A Princess Grows Up

My eldest daughter, Rochelle, had a huge impact on our lives when she was born. Life had changed; I was a father and had a bouncing, bubbly, energetic little girl to take care of. She didn't stay little for long. They never do. Three more little baby girls followed. Whew! My life was destined never to be the same, and I was embarking on an entirely new adventure, the never-ending saga of being a parent. It was five girls and me, and I was painfully outnumbered.

I think the odds were often better in the wilds with wild animals. The girls have always told me that although they know that I love them, they also believe that I wished one of them had been a son. I agree that I did desire a son, but I honestly would not have wanted to replace a single one of the girls—well, most of the time!

However, this perception may have translated into Rochelle striving very hard to be that son I never had. She was a tomboy from the word go. She grew into a tough, sinewy outdoors partner for me at the lodge. I once saw her single-handedly remove a 200-pound motor from the stern of one of the boats and drag it forward and onto the dock. In fact, at an early age all the girls would come to the Alaskan lodge and help out each summer, then leave just in time to go back to school. For many years, there wasn't a summer that all of them did not come and work very hard. I think many of the guests came to Alaska just to be around this lively crew. Each girl has awesome memories of those times that will be cherished forever.

Rochelle also had the flying bug, probably from all those summers watching the bush pilots and reveling in their stories when they returned from a fly-out. She loved to tag along when they had an empty seat and especially admired the pilots who "lived on the edge," because she is a born daredevil herself.

When she turned 14, she and I took flying lessons in California. It was tough and took about a year, but she persisted. She completed ground school, 40 hours of instructor training and flying hours and had only the written final exam to complete. She studied very hard for it. When she got to the training facility and began the test on the computer, word came in that an 11-year-old pilot had crashed, killing two people. The FAA reacted immediately and banned all persons under 16 from flying solo.

When Rochelle put her name into the FAA computer in preparation to take the test, an instructor came and asked her for her ID. When they determined she was only 14, they would not allow her to take the exam. She was confident she would have passed. This crushed Rochelle, because she had worked so hard to become a pilot. She had completed and passed all the requirements but was forbidden to finish her final examination and therefore was not allowed to fly. She had come very close to flying planes at a very young age.

I took flying lessons because I wanted to get my own license so that in case of an emergency situation, I could fly the planes out of trouble. At least that was the idea. Otherwise, I wisely leave all the flying to other bush pilots.

When Rochelle turned 16, she returned to the flight school, took the pilot training again, and this time she passed everything with "flying" colors. She is a natural pilot. She was literally born to fly, much like Jacob. That year she flew front seat with the pilots a couple of times, and then I let her fly the Cub, which was at a landing strip at Lake Clark near the lodge.

She was so excited. The Cub is the crème de la crème of Super Cubs and it was my baby. When Rochelle returned from her flight, she was still sky high. She rushed back to the lodge and found her mom. She crossed her first and second fingers in that universal bonding gesture and squealed, "Mom. The Cub and I were one. We were one! That was awesome. I love it!" Sharon, knowing the precarious life of a bush pilot in the wild, was thinking, *O Lord! Spare this child!*

There are a few women bush pilots in Alaska. A friend of mine was married to one, and I asked him how it went. He said that overall it was fine, but sometimes it was rather interesting. I asked him to explain and he told me the following:

He said, "Last year we had heard from the FAA that there was a huge storm coming in and lots of snow expected. They said to tie down all the airplanes on the south side of the airport so the snow blowers could avoid them and also it would provide more clearance for emergency landings. My wife hurried out and tied down our plane on the south side. A week later the same thing happened, but this time they wanted the planes moved to the north side. My wife rushed to the airport and again complied. Then a couple of days later she heard the announcement again, but the last of the instructions were garbled. My wife was frantic. She asked me, 'On which side of the airport should I park the plane, the north or south?' I thought for a moment, and then replied, 'Honey, why don't you just leave it in the hangar this time?' "

Jeremy Davis, a terrific man and wonderful Alaskan bush pilot, took Rochelle under his "wing." They would listen to crazy music and fly all over while he showed her the fine points of flying in Alaska. She would invariably come back from those trips pumped up, and it was obvious, she sincerely had a lifelong passion for flying. She and young pilot, Jacob, had both been infected with the same incurable affliction.

All the bush pilots had influenced Rochelle, but one in particular inspired her. Her name was Cinnamon and she was one of the few female bush pilots in Alaska. Even though she was only in her mid twenties, she was well known far and wide. Wherever she went, villagers flocked to her plane to see this "lady bush pilot with the flaming red hair." In one case, a native named Huggy Bear (so named because he was nearly killed by the fierce "hug" of a dying grizzly bear) took off his prized bear tooth necklace and presented it to Cinnamon.

She was a terrific pilot and I just knew that Rochelle, whose nickname as a little girl had been "sugar plum" would be the next Cinnamon. As I thought about it longer, I wondered if they would team up and, considering their names, lively personalities and beauty, become known as the "Flying Spice Girls."

Doors actually open easier, in some respects, for a woman pilot in Alaska if she is good at her craft. Consider this: You are a lonely trapper in the wilderness and need supplies flown in. Whom are you going to call to haul in your necessities, even though you will only get to chat with them for a few moments? Now, would it be a weathered, smelly, bearded, grouchy, pot-bellied male pilot or a good looking, well-manicured lady pilot—even if she were toting a .45? Yep, I could easily envision Rochelle having an incredible future flying in the Alaskan bush.

Here is a nugget for the ladies: In Alaska there are many more men than there are women, so the *odds* for women are good . . . but I'm here to tell you women, the *goods* may be odd!

GITS

"Let your guide be your conscience."

I affectionately refer to the "guides in training" as GITs. I did not play favorites. The lead guide at the time was Greg "Smashmouth" Smith, and he was ruthless on his trainees. I told Sharon, "He is made of twisted steel and masculine appeal, but has *no* religious zeal."

Smashmouth had been a middle linebacker in college football, a position made for those who love to mete out punishment. He was 6 feet 4 inches, 220 pounds, very muscular and as tough as they come. He was also one of the best guides I ever had, especially when it came to hunting and packing. This guy was a stud.

Fresh guides were mostly green and did not have a clue when they arrived just how quickly their decisions could become disastrous. Smashmouth was rough on them, and he needed to be. Mistakes in the unforgiving wild are often deadly. I did not want to bury one of them, one of the clients or one of the girls.

Rochelle had begged me to allow her to be a guide. She wanted to do more than just help out at the lodge and in the kitchen. Sharon, who was in charge of the lodge and kitchen staff, hated to let her go because Rochelle worked so hard cleaning, charming the guests, preparing the food and cooking, along with a host of other things. Most of all, Sharon just loved working with her daughters because they were so much fun. She and Rochelle had a great relationship and guests loved to kid with them at mealtime.

Sharon knew that Rochelle wanted to work with her dad as a guide along with the other guys. She knew how much Rochelle enjoyed flying out in the bush with clients, and she also knew that Rochelle ultimately had visions of a greater role in Alaskan Adventures. Consequently, Sharon knew that Rochelle wanted to prepare herself for that dream.

Rochelle could out-fish most of the guides by her early teens, so reluctantly I relented and gave in to her wish.

Rochelle completed the state requirements, got her CPR certificate and was issued an assistant guide license, which didn't permit her to work alone but did allow her to work for a Master Alaskan Fishing and Registered Hunting Guide—that being me. (My wife is the *master* and I am certifiably *registered*!)

First, I put Rochelle under the tough hand of Smashmouth. I gave him complete rein with her and he relished making her life difficult. I suppose I wanted to find out if Rochelle was serious or if she would tuck her tail and whimper off.

I was pretty sure she could cope. When our previous lodge had burned, we had to scramble to rebuild another one at our present location in time for opening of season. There had been some terrible flooding and much of our lodge and cabins were in standing water. The thawing snow, warming weather and intense rain had made most of the area a muddy quagmire.

I had flown in some beat-up sawmill machinery that ran on gas, managed to get it together and running, and we had set up shop. We began the tough task of cutting nearby gnarly pines, hauling logs by hand, making rough boards and rebuilding the outbuildings and upgrading the lodge.

Rochelle was working right alongside the rest of the crew and asking no quarter. I remember once, while standing on the second floor of the lodge and looking out over the garden area, seeing her struggling with some un-evenly hewn boards she was carrying on her neck and shoulders. Unexpectedly she stepped into a depression and fell face down into the sloppy mud, spraying water and the boards every which way.

I looked to make sure she wasn't hurt, and when I was satisfied she wasn't, I continued to watch to see what she would do. She raised her mud-spattered head out of the slop, shook the muddy water from her face and hair and tried to catch her breath. She lay there for a few moments and I could tell she was crying softly. She then took a deep breath, pulled herself up to her feet, stopped crying and looked around to determine if anyone had seen her.

She brushed some of the mud off her face, cleared her mouth and eyes of dirt and grime and slowly began the process of collecting the boards and repositioning them on her back and shoulders. I did not hear her once call for help or act as if she was going to quit her task. I had to smile inside. That was my girl, and she had some of our family steel inside.

Well, Smashmouth gave her all the grunt jobs and made sure she knew that being the boss's daughter meant nothing, and I am sure he felt she wouldn't make it. Like many young men working in a manly occupation, there was the usual banter, put-downs and poking fun at each other. Rochelle wasn't spared and got more than her share. Smashmouth was especially hard on her in front of the other guides, often making demeaning remarks to her.

I thought of stepping in a couple of times, but then I figured Rochelle probably needed to see the less glamorous side of young men when not at their Sunday best. Boys can act a lot different when they aren't trying to impress the ladies.

For a while it seemed that the more Rochelle persevered, the harder Smashmouth was on her. In spite of the rough treatment she got, she learned the nuances of being a good, safe Alaskan guide, and I gave her advice, as well. I was impressed because she stood her ground, and although I knew she occasionally vented with her mom late at night, she gritted her teeth and stuck it out during the day. She was certainly determined to prove herself in a world dominated by men.

A Woman Scorned

This all came to an abrupt halt when Smashmouth ultimately decided that Rochelle wasn't cutting the mustard. I am not completely sure whether he felt she was lacking as a guide or if Smashmouth just didn't want a young woman in a "man's world." At any rate, he stomped up to her one evening, rose up to his full height, pointed his finger at her face and bellowed, "You're fired! You ain't gonna guide with me anymore." Rochelle stood there in shock. Whoa! Smashmouth had just fired the boss's daughter—my daughter.

This really crushed Rochelle and seriously put me in a sour pickle. I didn't want to override the lead guide, especially with hunting season coming up. I had many hunters scheduled who were eagerly awaiting their adventure in the wilderness. If he quit I was in deep trouble, since most of the other guides there had to leave to get back to school before hunting season began, and none could hunt and pack like he could.

Smashmouth and I made a great hunting team, but I did not want to upset the family, either. Sharon was livid and let me have it double barreled in her frustration with Smashmouth. The other guides discreetly tried to stay out of it, but I could sense that they were divided in their opinions. I did not want to alienate the crew and I did not want to be disowned by my family. I thought with chagrin, *Just what am I going to do?*

Smashmouth was loyal to me as well. I knew that Smashmouth always had my back, even if it didn't appear that way at times. I was in a tough spot.

Rochelle had been doing double duty as a kitchen helper early and late with Sharon and the other girls and then training as a guide during the day. Now here she was back in the kitchen full-time, and she was fuming inside. She probably felt I had let her down, and she certainly believed she should not have been fired. The misery didn't stop there.

Smashmouth was very fussy about his food and he particularly hated Miracle Whip. He was especially resentful when Miracle Whip was used on his sandwiches instead of mayonnaise. (He obviously wasn't from the Deep South.) He would come storming into the kitchen and yell at the staff, "I don't want this sweet tasting Miracle Whip on my sandwich! I want real mayonnaise! I want my cheese put on this side and my lettuce this way and my ham here, and I want you to use mayonnaise, not that other junk. And when you finish, write my name on the bag so no one will eat my sandwich."

One of the attendant problems that arose out of this was that guests and other guides were starting to emulate him in making special requests from the kitchen, asking for a certain kind of cheese or no mayonnaise or no Miracle Whip, and so on. This resulted in the staff spending two and three times as long making all of these special sandwiches for the fishing trips and having to label all the bags. People would complain when theirs wasn't just so, and it was a hassle when lunchtime came and one client was across the river and

Salmon Barbeque By the River

another was up the lake and their "special" sandwiches were elsewhere because we could only keep them fresh in one or occasionally two coolers.

Now, trust me, I love to treat the guests to great food, and one of the greatest compliments I get every year is on the quality, quantity and sheer flavor I am able to provide. I have a professional chef who does most of the cooking and I am a fair cook myself, often preparing huge wildlife game dinners all over the country. At the lodge, I grow a variety of Alaskan "homegrown" vegetables and serve wonderful wild game dinners to the guests with numerous species of fish and big game.

I provide great meals on the field trips, as well, but those trips are not about food. The focus is on the awesome beauty of Alaska and the amazing wildlife. On these particular fishing trips, I would take the guests across Lake Clark, into a small bay, enter a wild rushing river, navigate up to some treacherous falls and provide them with an incredible experience.

They would be positioned near some rugged bluffs and rushing falls with a great view of salmon leaping out of the water, flying high into the air trying to find their way to the top, seeking a little crevice here, a tiny pool there, and ever struggling to get past all obstacles. Grizzlies would climb onto the rocks jutting into the falls and waylay the salmon fighting fiercely to return to the place of their birth. Foxes would linger nearby, patiently waiting for scraps. Eagles would soar in and snatch the fish. It was truly splendid, a memorable wildlife bonanza, and often clients would just set their poles down and watch the nature show.

Of course, once the salmon reached some of the deeper pools or mouths of connecting streams, the clients would enjoy some of the greatest fishing they had ever experienced. I loved it as each year more and more of the guests would catch and release these beautiful fish, release them to continue their incredible cycle of life.

Well, I guess that being the lead guide had in due course gone to Smashmouth's head. The girls in the kitchen were getting ready to mutiny, the crew was on a knife's edge and I was still fumbling for a solution. That was when Smashmouth came to my rescue. Yep, he made a critical error.

He thought it would be fun to play a little trick on Rochelle and me. You see, he loved habanero peppers. His family even grew them, so he would bring his own supply to the lodge every year and use them liberally on his food. No one else would even dare touch them. Habaneros are at the absolute top of the heat chain, a place that is well earned. It is an undeniable fact that too many habaneros, like too many birthdays, will kill a person!

Smashmouth decided to cut some habanero peppers into small pieces and put them into some seafood pasta that would be served to Rochelle and me at dinner. All of our guests and crew were there to enjoy the pasta, too, and the tables were full. Of course, only Rochelle's and my plates contained heat-seeking missiles.

We said our blessing for our tasty fare, and I noticed that everyone seemed to be glancing my way as I started in on one of my favorite dishes, Alaskan seafood fettuccine. I am at ease with getting curious stares, so I mentally waved it off and started wolfing down a couple of big bites. Rochelle was right next to me doing the same thing.

All of a sudden, both of us reacted in sheer agony. I have never felt anything so stingingly hot in my life. I thought I had swallowed a fully lit cigar. My throat and mouth were on fire, and Rochelle was floundering next to me. We were choking, gagging, jaws hanging wide open, taking those little short in–and-out puffs of breath, and I thought I was going to have a heart attack.

I was flailing about in search of water, ice, walk-in freezers, snow—anything cool. I was coughing and couldn't breathe deeply. My tongue felt as if it had been seared on a blazing hot barbecue grill. I was gasping and calling for help and Rochelle was carrying on in similar fashion. I needed the whole fire department, now!

It was then I saw through blurred vision that everyone was looking at me and laughing. Smashmouth was leading the way, slapping his thigh, snorting and belching like a well-slopped pig. As I continued to panic, my eyes watering, stumbling about and grasping my throat, most of those laughing quickly realized that this joke had gone far enough. They could see I was in real trouble and immediately jumped up and offered assistance, bringing water, setting us on a couch nearby and trying to calm us. I think our mouths burned for at least 15 minutes. I seriously think I came close to choking to death. Those things are scorching hot!

I think Smashmouth realized that his "joke" had been in poor *taste*, but he had known me long enough to learn that I can take it as well as I give it. I have often had fun teasing clients or picking on various staff members, to their dismay and/or amusement, and receiving the same, much to their delight. I didn't say anything to Smashmouth; however, my philosophy has been never to do anything that would actually hurt anyone, and usually that same credo is shared both ways.

Moose Turd Sandwiches

Well, if Rochelle had been "hot" before, she was a raging furnace now. Smashmouth had made Rochelle's life miserable for quite a spell, pulling some rather underhanded tricks on her, but now after putting burning coals in our mouths, he was public enemy number one. Rochelle surmised, correctly, I might add, that Smashmouth was fair game. So, Rochelle sweetly bided her time and, as we were soon to discover, would definitely have the last say.

She and Merilee, the next oldest daughter, snuck off into the brush near the lodge one morning and after awhile found what they sought. They discovered some prime fresh moose turds. Although moose are quite large, their droppings are relatively small, brownish green in color and shaped like fat Tootsie Rolls. Rochelle and Merilee carefully selected some "delicious" looking turds, secreted them in some paper and returned to the kitchen.

There they enlisted the help of the two youngest daughters, Kelly and Sunny, who were eager to assist. They took some very nice pieces of ham, selected the best slices of Swiss cheese, picked some crisp lettuce and carefully wrapped the moose turds inside of them, shaping and distributing them deftly throughout the sandwich. The turds had been so fresh they had not hardened and thus were deceivingly adaptable to their new home. Naturally, the girls slathered the bread with lots of mayonnaise and politely remembered to put Smashmouth's name neatly on his sandwich bag.

With their delightful plan in action, they enlisted one of their loyal sympathetic guides, Eric, to assist. They gave him a camera to take on the trip that day to photograph Smashmouth in his entire gourmet-eating splendor. They wisely kept me in the dark about their devilish plan. They couldn't help giggling throughout the day in anticipation of what they would learn upon the return of the crew from their day of fishing and feasting on delicious sandwiches so lovingly prepared.

Well, as providence would have it, I was sitting near Smashmouth when we decided to break for lunch. I grabbed one of the sandwiches and began munching and, as always, enjoying eating outdoors. Food just seems to taste better that way, and the splendor of our location only added to the ambience. I was gratefully feeling the soothing relief of giving my body some time to relax. I was lounging next to some blueberry patches loaded with big, round, ripe berries and I scooped handfuls to eat along with the fare. Ah, life doesn't get much better than that.

Soon I noticed that some of the other guides had edged closer to me and behind Smashmouth, and then from off to the side I saw another guide taking pictures of him. I could see that some of the clients were getting closer, too, and had smirks on their faces. What in Who-ville was going on?

Smashmouth seemed to be really enjoying his sandwich. I noticed it was pretty fat and full of good-looking ham, cheese and lettuce. He was chomping on it in complete satisfaction, and I was puzzled at the interest that was being shown him, although he was deliriously oblivious to it. I knew something was up because the guide with the camera kept taking picture after picture. I was getting very curious to see what was going to unfold.

I didn't have to wait long. When Smashmouth had devoured about a half of his sandwich, part of it slipped in his hand and one of the moose turds squirted out and fell in front of him onto the ground. My stomach turned inside out because I immediately understood that Smashmouth had been had big time, and I began uncontrollably laughing my silly head off. The other guides and clients began laughing hysterically too. I was giggling so hard I lay on my side and began to roll in the blueberries.

Smashmouth was stunned. He stared hard at the rest of his sandwich, and as full realization sank in, his eyes began to widen and his mouth dropped fully open, causing chewed up bits of ham, cheese and gooey moose turd lathered with mayonnaise to start spilling from his lips and onto his chin, clothes and the ground.

He lurched to his feet, shaking and trembling, and began yelling, "There are moose turds in my sandwich!" He drew his arm back and wildly tossed the sandwich as hard as he could into the air, pieces scattering everywhere, including some more moose turd chunks. He began retching, stumbling forward while bent over, coughing and belching, obviously trying to gag his food up from his stomach. He was foaming, spitting and muttering, "I ate moose turds, I ate turds! Turds, I tell you, I was eating turds! Someone put turds in my sandwich!"

The more we laughed, the madder he got. He kept stomping around, spitting and cussing, shaking his head and clenching his fists, and all the while gunky brown junk was drooling down both sides of his chin. He was so out of control I thought he might fall off the bank into the icy river.

Alternating hands, he would stick several curled fingers into his mouth, rotating them in a circular motion, trying to scoop out additional residue. Abruptly he straightened up, came to a halt and exploded, "I know who did this! A girl did this to me! I swallowed turds because of a girl!"

He turned and pointed a grungy, sloppy, wet finger in my direction. I grimaced when I saw a straggly piece of lettuce loosely attached to it, partially hanging down and swaying back and forth as he shook it at me. I mused at how long it would continue to hang onto that trembling finger. Smashmouth then curled his turd-dip coated lips and blurted loudly, "It was Rochelle who fed me those moose turds!"

Oh, gracious! By now, all of us were goners, weeping and laughing and pointing at Smashmouth and the moose turd pieces that were lying on the ground around him. My stomach was shaking so hard it hurt for several hours, but I didn't care. It was one of the funniest things I had ever seen, and I was thinking that it could not have happened to a more deserving person.

Instinctively, I knew he was right. He had been foiled by a girl. Of course it was Rochelle. Now, that was payback! And she had gotten the pictures to prove it.

Smashmouth didn't speak to me for a couple of days, but then he realized that people wouldn't respect him if he could play jokes on others and not be willing to be a good sport when the tables were turned.

During the ensuing hunting season, he and I spent a lot of time tracking and packing game in the bush, in cold tents with clients or waiting for clients. We laughed and laughed about his favorite sandwich. Yes, sir, it doesn't matter what you put in them as long as you use lots of mayonnaise!

Well, I reinstated Rochelle as a guide starting the next week and she had a new spring in her step. I must say that Smashmouth took it in stride, and the tension in the lodge dispersed like cash from a teenager. My family and I have spent more than a few enjoyable evenings reveling in retelling the incident.

Rochelle continued to learn quickly and became a darn good fishing guide, enchanting the clients, running boats through treacherous rivers, cleaning and filleting fish and working alongside other guides and some rough characters in the process.

The guides still didn't give her any slack, but I didn't worry too much about her anymore because she never failed to give as good as she got. Nevertheless, I kept a wary eye on things. I may have been born on a Tuesday, but trust me, it wasn't last Tuesday.

As for Smashmouth, he had worked for me for four years and was one of the best guides I ever had. However, after that season he went to California and got into the shelving business. I have often wondered if those moose turds "shelved" my hunting warrior, but more than likely, he just moved on in life.

I do know that when I get to visit or see him someday we will share some laughs and maybe even a sandwich or two, imbued with mayo, of course, and spanking clean of anything remotely related to the Alaskan moose.

The Last Laugh!

Chapter 9 – The Caveman Within

Chapter Nine

The Caveman Within

"I may be schizophrenic, but at least I have each other."

J ack London said, "The proper function for all men is to live, not just exist." A wilderness adventure is a great environment for doing just that. It is an intense experience that can make you truly live, discover who you are and become acutely alive, sometimes in unexpected ways.

"You just don't understand us, Rocky. Men and women are different. We are from Venus and you are from Mars." An earlier off-season conversation I'd had with my wife was sifting through my utterly relaxed brain.

I was completely at ease because I was in my sanctuary. I was in the wilderness of Alaska, floating alone down a wild river. There wasn't a theatre, museum or real city within two hundred miles. A cell phone would have been useless in this remote spot. I had severed connections to civilization. I loved it. This setting was as close to heaven on earth as any place I had ever known. I sighed and took it all in. I was at peace in my heart.

But Sharon's words kept intruding: "I just don't understand you sometimes."

Well, I sure don't understand her or the four daughters most of the time, I was thinking. Why was that? I could read the minds of wild animals, or so I often thought. I could sense when they would run or charge or what direction they would go. Many times I had said to one of the guests, "Here is what that bear (or moose or caribou) is going to do. Now just watch and wait . . ." Sure enough, I would be right—well, most of the time.

I could do this without ever having had an actual conversation with an animal (a four-legged one, that is). Except Roscoe, of course. Roscoe was the largest moose I had ever hunted. He had outwitted others and me for years. I had become fascinated with him, and somehow he had infiltrated my dream world. Dreams in which I am sure we spoke—at least, I hope they were dreams.

Sharon's words cut back into my thoughts. "Could you just explain yourself in a way that helps me understand a little more about the male ego, dear? Just a little, please? There are six of us in our family, you know, and five of us are girls. We need help understanding the oddball—you!"

She did? Now, why was that necessary? I lived by a very reliable credo: If at first I don't succeed, just do it the way Sharon told me to!

I didn't see my ego or manly self as particularly complicated. I still enjoyed looking at Sharon, my lovely wife of several decades. I liked to eat red meat, preferred sleeping in a big bed without 38 stuffed animals, gnawed on wooden toothpicks after a good meal, found tap water tasty and sufficient and worked hard to provide for the family. What was odd about that?

I didn't like to rattle on about someone's feelings or worry about what day the fall colors were supposed to be worn, and naturally, I appreciated the abilities of a good hound dog. Now, tell me, how simple can one get?

You never know what is around the next bend . . .

Of course, I agonized about how the local football and bas-basketball teams would fare.

I was drifting aimlessly downstream, boat motor off, and it was a lovely Alaskan day. The crystal clear blue sky was limitless, the air was cool, eagles were in treetops eyeing the river for fish and beavers were slapping their tails on the water warning others of my whereabouts. It was one of those priceless times you would like to capture and put in a bottle—put it in several bottles and take back to California, to be sipped slowly on crowded freeways.

As the boat continued to drift, my mind drifted to other things. I gazed at the wild, rugged landscape, feeling that in spite of its seemingly random structure, there was still a sense of order. I had an overwhelming sensation that this cruel land, with all its ferocious animals and constant struggle for man and beast alike just to survive, somehow held within it healing secrets, special balms that spoke to you louder each time as you began to pay attention and really listen. Adventures here were almost always healthy.

In direct contrast, man-made attempts at adventure seemed unhealthy, at least on many levels. Men sought various ways to get that adrenaline rush, through gambling, road racing, fighting, violent video games, drugs, adultery and similar activities. These did not seem to have the same effects as real wilderness adventures and were often destructive. Maybe women needed an adrenaline rush, too, but it appeared to me that men and boys sought these pursuits in greater earnest and greater numbers.

To my way of thinking, without healthy adventures to test their masculinity, those same boys will struggle to become healthy men. Is this one of the prime differences between the sexes? If so, how could I explain it to Sharon? How could I possibly demonstrate this to her or describe it to her? I could just hear her: "Why do you need to catch a big salmon, Rocky? Why do you want to face wild animals or fly in dangerous weather in that small bush plane? Why do you challenge nature? Think about your family and why you have to prove yourself."

"Yes, dear," I mentally replied, "why indeed?"

Why do men need challenges? I reflected back on childhood. I was constantly fighting, wrestling, chasing and being chased by my brothers and other kids. We would see who could throw a rock the farthest, ride a bike the fastest, jump the widest part of the creek, punch the hardest and endure the most pain, or anything else we could imagine as long as we were testing our skills and toughness. I have frequently watched young cats, dogs and other animals do the same, having mock fights and training themselves for future battles.

I believe it is more than that. I have a strong sense that it is deeper than training for future confrontation. I think a lot of inner awareness, social interaction skills and self-identity are formed during this period. It is a time of learning how you will do under stress or pressure, learning how to cope. Picking yourself up after losing a fight, persevering and not quitting is healing.

It is not about whipping the town bully; it is about taking him on, win or lose. It teaches you how to survive in the real world and not give up. You discover what it means to be a man. You learn how to laugh at yourself through success and failure.

To me, this is an essential part of the growth of a man. Our society seems to frown on these youthful exhibitions of force. They want our young men to act like their distaff counterparts. In some schools, boys are no longer even allowed to play tag. They are being told, in so many words, to act like girls because by some current definitions, boys and girls are deemed the same.

No wonder then, when boys grow up, they have never learned how to be a man. Inside, though, I believe many long for the adventures they never had and often develop addictions to compensate.

I should write all this down. Does this happen to you? For us men, just a few reflective moments alone in the right environment, when we are able to think clearly without distractions, and voila, we can solve even the world's toughest problems. Well, here I was, floating along on this quiet river and my mind was churning out all this wonderful wisdom. At least, it always seems so terrific and logical at the time. Why does it never sound as profound when I try to explain it all later?

I guess I was thinking that in America, young men have lost their rite of passage. Turning 18, getting a driver's license or physical involvement with a girl does little to make this transition valid or special, yet those seem to be our major markers.

Many cultures make a big deal of a boy becoming a man, and there are various traditions and adventures that accompany this critical process, sometimes over months or years, including leaving boys alone in strange places like faraway forests or remote islands with few supplies, just to see if they will survive.

Consider this: a Massa tribesman must put a spear into a lion before he is elevated to a warrior. I am not suggesting this particular tradition, but I am behind the idea of a young man being truly tested. Manhood should be earned. When young men learn they can overcome, they face life with a positive outlook. They are less likely to become victims. They develop a belief in themselves.

The boys in these cultures rarely fail to survive, and then they *thrive* thereafter. Sometimes it involves a hunt with the men, various tests or other male bonding rituals, or even a study curriculum of important values and disciplines. To those cultures I say, "Kudos." You got it. Did we lose this concept somewhere along the way in America? Most cultures still recognize this period as very significant, but do we?

"Don't forget the candles for the double fudge cake, dear, the one with Beavis and Butthead on it. After all, it is his 16th birthday." Yeah, that'll do it.

On the other hand, I admit I didn't always understand my girls either, especially during their teenage years. Now that was double trouble, wrong age and wrong gender. Was it really that or was masculinity getting in the way? What was I missing? Maybe girls need adventure too.

Maybe they need to stretch themselves in similar ways on a more sensitive or verbally challenging platform. I don't know, but being in love seems to be their purest version of adventure. Becoming vulnerable and opening their heart and sharing. Talk about scary. Whew! I think I would rather swim with man-eating sharks.

No matter what your location, eventually, it is time for your daily visit to the throne, but there are no facilities readily available in wild Alaska and certainly weren't on the aluminum boat. However, it is a fairly wide and stable vessel, so I set about making the proper preparations and clothing adjustments and sat down on the back gunwale of the boat near the motor.

Now, can someone tell me the reason that when something crazy is going to happen, it unerringly selects the exact second you are at your most vulnerable, the most exposed? Has that happened to you? Someone opens a door at the precise wrong moment? You are shooting your mouth off and the microphone is on, or the person being ridiculed has slipped unknowingly behind you? A strap or bag or suitcase breaks or flops open at the most embarrassing time? Well, there I was contemplating life and minding my own business, when out of nowhere I heard a loud angry roar.

The boat had been drifting backwards, and I quickly whipped my head around and looked in the direction of the ferocious growl I had heard farther downstream. The sight I saw amazed me. A huge grizzly bear had just finished killing a grown moose and was lingering at the water's edge. He must have surprised the doomed animal as the moose was swimming across. The grizzly had seen the boat after I drifted around a bend and then came fully into his view. He was only about 100 yards off, and the boat was drifting straight at him in the moderate current.

Initially, I was transfixed, due in part to my situation but also to the suddenness of this incredible encounter. I could not move very well due to the blue jean cuffs around my ankles, but I didn't feel especially in danger. I tried to think. My handgun was tucked away safely in the gear, but it would take too long to get to it. I had not brought a rifle. I knew that the only shooting I would be doing at this bear, should that be necessary, would be a "moon shot." I seriously doubted that would faze him. Course, he might die laughing.

I looked at the bear. He was so powerful it amazed me. This was not a small calf he was finishing off but a young mature moose, probably weighing nearly 800 pounds, which was likely near the bear's own weight. The dying moose was bloody, wet and slippery. The grizzly had his powerful jaws clamped on the back neck area of the moose and was backing very slowly up the slight incline of the grassy riverbank.

His teeth were clenched tightly and he was struggling mightily to get the animal out of the water and up the bank. He would back up a couple of inches, and then scrunch himself up and jerk backwards very hard with his head, neck and shoulders. He had all four paws and every claw gripping and planted firmly in the riverbank to provide support. He would grunt with each heave and then look at me and snarl menacingly, occasionally shaking his head vigorously like an angry bulldog.

Incredibly, he was actually moving this moose up the bank, inch by inch. His mouth was dripping with water and blood, and he was growling more loudly as he saw the boat drifting closer. It was obvious that he thought I was after his kill, and he was letting me know in his own graphic language that he would not stand for it. His wet fur accentuated the rippling of his muscles as he put all of his strength into getting the moose away from the river and into some nearby brush.

I became so entranced with the antics of this beast and the intensity of this wilderness saga that I almost forgot where I was. It was as if I was at a picture show. I just sat dumbfounded on the boat, all the while drifting toward this angry, growling grizzly, this giant bear that was getting madder by the second.

Then the thoughts that had been racing through my head previously began to stir me. It seemed my manhood was being discussed and challenged. Explanations requested. Right? For me, a big part of real manhood was stepping up to the plate when needed, especially if some measure of force was required. I was becoming annoyed by watching what I felt to be a predator killing one of the most majestic animals of the north. Predators were obsessively protected while moose weren't. I could feel my blood rising, my heart pumping and my anger beginning to tighten my jaw and curl my lips. Yes, ladies, my manhood was starting to rumble.

My lower brain was beginning to take control. I looked at the bear calmly, clenched and bared my own cigar stained teeth and knew exactly what I had to do. When I

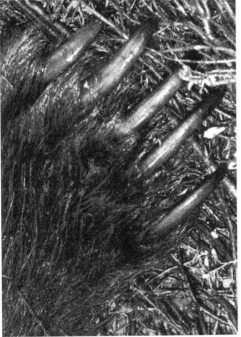

got close enough, I was going to explode out of this boat and charge this bear! He snarled at me and understood. There was no referee. This was not about fairness or being nice. This was about him and me.

This was about life. It was about proving who was in control, who was king of this domain. He knew it and I knew it. He wasn't going to run and leave his kill. It was the law of the jungle. He would fight to the death for the life he had taken. I deliberately shook the pants loose from around my ankles.

I bent down carefully, keeping my gaze on the bear, and took my knife out of its scabbard, which was attached to the belt on the discarded pants. By now, the boat had drifted very close to the bank. The bend in the river created a reverse current near the water's edge, and this along with the swirling wind had slowed the boat to a basic standstill. The boat became almost motionless in the shallow water, roughly parallel to the bank and only about 15 yards from the dead moose and its killer. I stood there in the clear, cool air wearing nothing but a shirt and shoes and a vicious, sarcastic scowl. I was holding the sharp, long-bladed knife in my right hand. I stared at the bear and he glared at me. No quarter was asked for and none was given.

As I stood there, unkempt hair waving in the breeze, legs wide, feet braced, eyes intently focused, every muscle coiled and ready for action, mercifully the more civilized side of my brain began to break through. I smiled to myself as insane thoughts swirled in my head. I almost laughed when I considered how puzzling it would be for anyone who came upon this scene and found me, seminude and clawed to pieces.

You see, I was under no illusions about who would ultimately win this contest. Those who discovered me would likely never be able to figure out how a grizzly had gotten my pants off. If they examined them and saw they weren't torn, then the obvious conclusion would be that I had taken them off myself. The question that followed would be, "Why on earth did he take his pants off?"

Naturally, the next logical question would be, "Why did he leave his handgun untouched and instead opt for his knife?" I knew that no one would ever understand why a partially nude, poorly armed, yet very experienced guide was found in this condition. As I stood there, in my gut I instinctively knew the answers to these questions, and maybe I am mistaken, but I suspect many of the men reading this will also understand.

In fact, those answers seemed plain to me at that moment, sort of like things that make sense in dreams but would be incomprehensible to my wife and girls later. If I lived through this, it would be interesting to try to explain it to them. Actually, it was going to prove very interesting to try to explain it to anyone!

The grizzly had gotten the moose to a more level spot and was hovering over it and being very protective of his kill. He was just over 15 yards away, straddling his kill, and he kept his gaze squarely fixed on me. He growled, roared and snapped his head forward slightly, baring his teeth and shaking his head and long jaws. With every shake, the water and blood clinging to his fur were splattering onto the moose and grass around the bear.

His eyes seemed small compared to his head and body, and they emitted an intense golden glint like sparks from a hot fire. He was letting me know he was not afraid of taking me on and was contemplating his own charge. We were at an impasse, each trying to read the other. Then it hit me: He was waiting for me to decide whether I wanted to commit suicide.

My mind flashed back with a jolt to a time I actually had stabbed a bear. In that situation, I had been kidding around with a hunter after he had killed a bear. I had skinned the bear and rolled it over onto its back. As I stared at it, I instantly had this nutty idea. I grabbed a knife (the same one I now held) and with a mock war yell, leaped high in the air, landed on top of the bear and plunged the knife into its upper chest as hard as I could. The hunter almost died laughing at the sight. I laughed, too—in surprise, because when I saw how little I had penetrated the chest of the bear, I was stunned.

The razor sharp knife had gone in no more than an inch. An inch! Those rib and breastplate bones were thick and tough! Moreover, that dead bear lay unmoving on the ground, providing solid support for me to stab his chest, and he was minus his thick fur, to boot. He was not writhing or resisting and was smaller than the very alive beast that was waiting impatiently for me to get on with this deadly game I was playing. Reality was starting to set in.

I glanced at the knife in my hand and thought about how I looked standing there. I could just imagine someone in another boat rounding the bend and seeing me. I am sure they would not have believed what they saw, which was a large, crazy, Alaskan bearded man fronting off a much larger grizzly and holding nothing but a knife, with both combatants wearing nearly the same outfit, the one in which they were born. The shocked boaters would have either timidly offered help or turned around and sped off to saner regions.

I began to reflect. Was this insanity? Had the wilderness affected my mind? Or was this a primitive reaction that had been aroused in my brain, a deeper mirror into my masculinity? Did I have some weird wish to die and, if so, to do it in a fashion that would make a statement about who I was? I knew it would be a statement that might be difficult for friends and family to fathom. It certainly would not provide closure for them. I could just imagine the headlines in the Anchorage Daily News:

CRAZY SEMI-NUDE GUIDE FIGHTS GRIZZLY TO THE DEATH WITH KNIFE!

Story continued on page 2 . . .

". . . The results of the encounter were predictable. Long-time, well-known Alaskan guide Rocky McElveen was found dead early yesterday on the banks of the remote Holitna River. He was partially clothed, mauled badly and chewed to pieces, his bloody knife lying only a few feet from him. The fresh, mangled remains of a moose were nearby. His boat, containing a fully loaded handgun along with some of his discarded clothes, was discovered several miles downriver. Fish and Game personnel and State Troopers are investigating, but are greatly perplexed as to what happened. They are asking anyone having the slightest idea, or even someone with any recent encounter with McElveen, to come forward and hopefully shed some light . . ."

I wish I could say as I stood there contemplating the next move, that wife and family were paramount in my thoughts. Honestly, though, that was not a primary concern in my thinking. Maybe that is because I have learned that if you go too far in worrying about consequences, you run the risk of being paralyzed by fear, worrying more about failure than the task at hand. If your focus is on what will happen if you miss an important shot that could win the championship for your team, and how they will react, then you probably will miss the shot.

Nope, I like to forge ahead with the firm belief that I will succeed, that in spite of all the odds I will find a way to survive. I think that, too, is a part of becoming a man—developing confidence in who you are—and that is hard to do without living through and taking on some challenging obstacles. What better way is there to accomplish that than to experience wilderness adventures?

Yep, my thinking was on a more basic level, namely, that no matter how confident I felt as I charged this formidable beast, I was not going to prevail. Even more basic, what was the purpose? I would take him on if my child's life was at stake, of course, but the moose I had originally wanted to defend was already dead. The real reasons I was still considering fighting this grizzly were all about proving my manhood, being tough, having guts, personal pride, intense curiosity and primal instinct, and yes, I wanted to test myself against this bear, mano a mano.

I had always wondered how David of the Bible had killed a bear and a lion with his bare hands. I wanted to be David.

I was very curious about how this deadly fight would affect me, how it would go down, how my body and mind would react, and I even pondered how the sensation of dying would feel. Even as these morbid thoughts filtered their way through my consciousness, I also realized that every part of me was vibrant with life. Every fiber of my entire body was tingling and pulsating with excitement.

My senses were razor sharp and I could hear and smell things I normally could not.

I noticed a small white spot on the bear's black nose and a patch of missing fur on his side, probably from another fight. I was aware of some geese honking and flying somewhere off in the distance, and I could hear a mosquito buzzing near my left side, intent on some blood-letting of his own, probably thrilled at this big uncovered treasure trove he had discovered. I didn't care; I was supercharged and felt powerfully alive. All these things were affecting me and preparing me for battle. I clearly understood the message, and strangely, as I contemplated the next step, I deeply wanted this battle—I wanted to engage this enraged bear.

Without further ado, the grizzly let out an incredibly loud roar, shaking his whole body as he did so, the water still dripping from his beautiful, long, golden fur. He was tired of waiting. He wanted action. At this, my mind filled with a sudden rage. I shook from the intensity of it. I felt a rush of anger surge through me with an off-the-chart intensity. It was such a powerful emotion that it surprised me.

Then, from my gut, I had a compelling desire to meet his roar with one of my own, and a piercing, rasping snarl exploded from my lips. The time for waiting had ended. I drew back the hand holding the knife and held it high behind my head, blade pointed at the bear. I rocked my weight backwards in preparation to leap forward out of the boat. This was it. My insane war with this mammoth monster was about to begin.

At that very moment, everything went into slow motion; in fact, the entire scene seemed to come to a complete standstill. Then, shockingly, somewhere in the deep recesses of my brain, I heard a small and frail, but very clear voice that sounded eerily like a young child. I will never forget the words I heard: "Why are you angry at the bear, Rocky?"

What? Huh? Who is asking that? I stopped, jerked my head around and searched frantically for the source of the voice, but no one was there. Instantly I knew why. That voice had come from within. Why was I angry at the bear? What a silly thing to figure out now. Or was it? I forced myself to remain calm and try to understand this.

Sure, I was angry and the bear was angry. So what! But the question continued to mock me. Okay, I reasoned, I wasn't really angry at the bear. He had not done anything to me. He was just being who he was, a ferocious killer. I was not really angry with him. If that was the case, then why was I angry at all?

The truth began to pierce my heart. It was as if in that moment of confrontation with the grizzly, all the pain and injustices I had suffered and harbored during my life had promptly balled up and then, in an irrationally compressed fashion, had become needle sharp and focused their full resentment, hurt and frustrations into one powerful laser beam of hate that was directed squarely at this animal. The grizzly and this confrontation had become the retaliation outlet for deep hurt within my life.

I was stunned. I stared at the bear and completely relaxed my body, even dropping the knife into the boat. The sound of the knife hitting the metal boat caused the bear to rear up on his hind legs and glare at me, sniffing the air intently. Quickly, he sensed that something had changed with me, but he didn't know what it was. He gave me one more ear-splitting roar. I just looked at him and smirked. He was only 15 yards away and could have covered the distance in a flash.

I still needed to show that I was a man, though. This had not only been about anger. Primitive instincts had been tapped, and the things I had mentioned earlier were still important to me, to my male psyche. I still had pride, and my masculinity ached for recognition.

Therefore, I turned my back on the bear and casually got dressed. Somehow, inside, my disdain for this beast made me feel even stronger and bigger than charging the bear would have. I started the outboard and motored on down the river very much at peace. I never looked back at the bear. I knew in my heart that I had left a lot of baggage on that riverbank. I did not want to see it again.

I can only surmise the consternation the bear must have felt. He probably bragged to his next hoped-for female companion, "Yeah, I bagged me this moose and was getting ready for a feast when one of those weird stubby human-things floated up on a couple of wide shiny trees stuck together. This idiot took off some of his fur and he smelled awful. He then made a great display of flashing around his one puny claw! He was about ready to get his ticket punched when I decided to give him a break. I gave him one of my famous growls and he dropped his claw and high-tailed it outta there! Yeah, baby, if you want a real he-bear, I'm your grizzly!"

As I traveled downriver, I wondered how frequently built-up anger and resentment winds up being poured out on an innocent person or trivial situation. I have heard of episodes where people have been killed on the freeway due to road rage. Is it worth killing someone over a perceived insult of being cut off in traffic? A policeman told me that a man shot his neighbor dead because the neighbor's sprinkler had gotten his car wet. Maybe I am mistaken, but I believe men resort to deadly violence more than women do. Anger management can be valuable, but finding ways to prevent that anger from building up in the first place would be phenomenal.

Do you suppose that we are stifling our young men and not teaching them to become real men? Real men who are gentlemen, who are tolerant and who use sports, exercise, excursions into nature and hunting and fishing to release their natural aggressions and develop a healthy manhood. Our children are born needing beneficial outlets. What better way is there than challenging them in the wilderness?

I firmly concluded it is better to investigate the real causes for frustrations, to discover their true sources and find proper solutions and healthy ways to cope. Maybe that was what my wife was referring to. I know she never did quite grasp my tortured explanations to her very horrified inquiries.

Honestly, I think there are several good, rational reasons for my actions, and a couple that are more emotionally based in the primal core nature of a man. Sadly, this aspect of how men and women are different is not discussed with much insight in many arenas. Maybe it should be. Maybe for boys, young men and even mature men, it would be very helpful to discover more about what is hidden in the nether regions of a man's heart.

Maybe women are energized, too, when they experience an adventure with their man or when he relates an adventure to them, especially if it involves defending them. Then maybe they feel protected and safe, something that is very important to most women. In turn, they reveal their soul and energize their man with unconditional love. This makes him feel like a tough, strong man ready to take on the world for his lady, and she feels like a cherished woman. However, he may be unable to accomplish that at a significant level until he has first learned how to be a man.

When he does, I suggest it is less about specifically understanding each other and more about loving the differences and accepting them. As for me, I love it when my wife simply makes me feel big—the bigger the better—and believe me, women know how to build up their man. Sadly, both husbands and wives are experts at tearing each other down. Why not use the same skill in reverse. It will work wonders. My wife loves it when I treat her like my princess and guard her like my queen.

A healthy man can give his woman the one thing she craves even more than understanding: real love from a real man. I love cheesecake, but haven't a clue how it is made, and may not be so fond of it if I did. Completely understanding your mate may not be necessary or productive. To me, a little mystery keeps the intrigue alive.

I think a woman should be all woman, and men, real he-men, without apology. The wilderness is one place where healthy adventures often result in peeling off those layers and uncovering the true man or woman within that is longing to emerge and invigorate their lives. The first step of that journey, of course, is yours.

A woman friend of mine read a raw script of this chapter. I wanted to get her reaction. She said, "I don't get it."

That is my point *exactly*. This chapter contains a lot of information about a man that could be enlightening and beneficial, if understood better.

I know that when I returned to my family, I had a real appreciation for what God has given me. I enjoyed the warm embraces of the wife and kids and knew that I would have been a fool to give this up for my personal war with the bear, which in reality was my personal war within.

I grinned at the girls as they jumped up and asked excitedly, "Daddy, Daddy, did anything scary happen this summer?" I was very happy to reply, "Not really. Well, sorta . . . Do you want to hear some stories?" "Yes! Yes!" they replied, dragging me to the couch, holding me captive and encircling me tightly to hear the latest adventures.

Yes, it was good to be with family again. I keenly realized I had two loves, the wilderness and my family. I hope I never have to part with either.

Chapter Ten

Nimrod, The Mighty Hunter-Warrior

"Red meat is *not* bad for you; fuzzy green meat is bad for you."

Life at our remote lodge is more complex than just guiding and fishing or the quest for self-revelation. Sometimes I think those activities are no more than a sidebar. The familial setting, bonding and the enjoyment of each other in a wilderness world without pretense are all quite remarkable, I will admit. Nevertheless, before I continue, I want to introduce you to another warrior and some of the amazing little animals that we interact with.

In both of my books, I have related harrowing events that have happened to me or clients, including stories of angry charging grizzlies, plane crashes and other brushes with death in the Alaskan wilderness. However, there are smaller creatures that are an integral part of our life in the wild too.

I had purchased for Kelly, my second to youngest daughter, a beautiful Jack Russell Terrier. We named him Nimrod, which means "mighty hunter-warrior." This dog was true to his name and loved to chase all types of small critters. He was an incredible digger and he would often nearly disappear below ground while foraging for gophers and rats in their underground dens.

When he was still a young pup, I decided to take Nimrod to the Alaskan lodge. He took an instant liking to Alaska and his newfound freedom, and the guests took an instant liking to him. He had boundless energy and there were no fences to imprison him there. Every squirrel, rabbit, weasel, otter, fox or any other animal his size (or less) was fair game. He loved the water and would often jump in and paddle furiously, chasing anything he could see.

Upon returning from a hard day of fishing with the clients, we would take the fish down by the dock near the water's edge to clean them. We would fillet and prepare them either for a tasty supper or to be packaged in air-sealed plastic bags for the guests to take home with them. Back home, they would cook or barbecue the fillets, using their favorite recipes, and enjoy them with friends, all the while relating thrilling accounts of their adventures in the last frontier and the *really* big ones they had caught and *released.*

As we cleaned the fish, we would toss the heads and inedible parts into the water. This attracted birds and other fish, and invariably drew a group of lively otters that lived near the lodge. These beautiful animals are playful, agile, sleek and fun to watch.

Otters are from the *Mustelid* or weasel family of mammals and are the smallest marine mammals in North America. Inland otters in Alaska are commonly referred to as North American river otters, but that is a fairly recent moniker. River or land otters are generally smaller than their cousin, the sea otter; however, some would disagree that there is a real difference between these otters.

They make this claim notwithstanding demonstrable variances in behavior and size. Naysayers are of the opinion that those variables are solely a function of differing habitat, and they might have a point. It is similar to the discussion regarding the coastal brown bear and the interior grizzly, in which an invisible line drawn arbitrarily many miles inland has somehow become the defining demarcation for determining the classification of a brown bear. I guess, depending on what side of the line a brown or grizzly bear may occupy at any given moment, they can instantly change classifications!

Therefore, as the argument goes, an inland (grizzly) bear isn't really another type of bear; he has simply been raised in a predominantly harsher climate and his body naturally responds to cope with it. Consider this: Identical twins are born. One is raised solely in affluence in Beverly

Hills, California, and the other is raised in a poor hut in Africa. Might they act and appear different as adults?

Well, all otters play like kids, rolling around, wrestling, splashing water, toying with live prey, swimming in circles, and they love to spin their bodies on the surface. This spinning motion is hard to describe. To the naked eye, it almost appears that their heads and tails don't even touch the water as they spin. On land, they often run and then slide on their belly for up to 20 or more feet on mud or ice, or down embankments reaching speeds of 20 miles per hour or more.

In the water, they are expert swimmers and can dive for up to four minutes. They are carnivores and eat frogs, fish, shellfish, small birds and anything else they can catch. Otters can be fierce and have been known to kill beavers and take over their dens to raise their own young. Their pups are born blind and can't see for several weeks, so the otter mom has her hands full raising her pups and keeping them safe.

They have little fat on them, but stay warm in freezing water due to the unbelievable density of their fur. They have 600,000 hairs per square inch! In comparison, humans have about 20,000 hairs on their entire head. It is because of the otter's luxurious fur that they were almost hunted into extinction.

It is a special treat to watch otters eat. They select a tasty morsel, twist over and float on their backs. They put the food on their stomach, which serves as a mobile table. Course, I've seen some large clients of mine do the same. Otters are very resourceful and will take rocks, float on their backs, place the rocks on their stomachs and use their front paws to smash clams and other crustaceans into the rocks to break the shells apart. The "clicking" noises created can be heard for long distances.

If the portion of food they are eating is too large, they take it to shore to eat; if not, they will drift casually along, munching on their food as if they didn't have a care in the  world. That could not be further from the truth. Bears, wolves, coyotes and eagles are voracious predators of small animals, including weasels and young otters, and otter pups are at the top of their list of delicacies.

Now, eagles are simply awesome to watch. They have a wingspan of up to seven feet or more, and claws and talons that are sharp, strong and curved. Their upper beak is raked and perfectly suited to ripping the flesh of their prey. When they dive, they begin with a steep plunge and then level off and come in on a shallower plane, with perfect precision.

They thrust their talons into the water at just the right spot, stabbing swiftly into the back and sides of the fish, locking on with a deadly grip. Then, with a powerful sweeping motion of their wings, they lift their catch out of the water and soar off with their booty.

The reason eagles level off and glide in low over the top of the water is that they cannot afford to plunge into the water and get their wings soaked, as many other birds do. If that happens they can't easily fly again until they reach shore or find something floating to climb on in order to dry off and provide a better launching pad. They can swim by using their wings in a paddling motion, but if they are caught too far from land, they can tire and might die.

Eagles are able to insert or retract their talons at will, but if they are hungry and have picked on too large a fish, once they latch on and stick their talons in deeply, they may not want to let go soon enough. If the fish has twisted quickly and dived toward the bottom, the eagle may not be able to make a quick enough release. If that happens, the fish can literally drag them under water and drown them. (I actually witnessed this once, to my shock.) I was in a boat and moving along, but for the short time I was able to watch, I never saw the eagle surface.

I read somewhere that a large eagle can lift only about four pounds into the air, but I personally would dispute that. I have seen them take some pretty large fish that sure looked a lot bigger than four pounds, and after many years as a fishing guide, I can judge fish weight fairly well.

Needless to say, I easily become attached to the small animals near the lodge and get very disgusted with anyone who harms them. However, sometimes I have to let nature take its course.

One day I was lounging in a chair near the water with Nimrod nearby, catching a rare few moments to recharge and taking in the sights, when I noticed a large bald eagle circling high above. I looked with dismay toward the smaller otters, but they had already spotted the eagle. That is one of the advantages of floating on your back. You can see the sky. I keep telling Sharon that lying on my back in the middle of the day is only a simple exercise in safety.

My thoughts reflected back to another time when I had watched an eagle dive and grab a mother weasel close to the lodge. I had watched in disbelief and sadness as the weasel screamed, screeched and twisted, the eagle's claws gripping and piercing her during the ascending flight. Weasels are thought to be the meanest hunters in the world, pound for pound, but this poor mother was no match for the mighty eagle; she had kids of her own to feed.

I knew it was a mother weasel because we had discovered the entire orphaned pack of them under our equipment room, and she was the proud matriarch of quite a litter. Weasels are stunning little animals. They belong to the same family as otters and ferrets, but are only 7 to 14 inches long and resemble a longer, slender version of a mouse. They hunt mostly in the early evening or at night.

In snowy, colder climates such as that in Alaska, they turn white in winter to blend in and are tabbed as ermine. Their entire fur turns white except the tip of their tail. Often predators chasing them in the snow get obsessed with snapping at the little dark, darting tip of the tail and completely miss the feisty little weasel/ermine camouflaged with the snow.

Weasels eat about 25 percent of their weight each day and love mice. They are probably the best "mousers" (mice catchers) on the planet. They are fierce hunters and can easily kill much larger prey than themselves. On farms, they are famous for killing chickens. I can testify directly to their ferocity because I once watched in amazement as an overmatched squirrel was cornered by a weasel. The weasel destroyed the defenseless squirrel faster than I ever would have thought possible.

I loved having them around the lodge and appreciated their keeping down the mouse population. When their mom was taken by the eagle, I trapped a couple of her forsaken litter and, with some patience, was able to make them into lodge pets. After a week or two of feeding them, they would happily sit in my pocket, occasionally peeking out and sniffing for more food. They particularly loved to eat bloody scraps of caribou, and interestingly, they loved dog food.

In fact, that is how we initially caught one of the weasels. Nimrod's dog food was kept in a barrel, but the top was not secured. The weasels would climb in through the top and munch away. Eventually the food in the bag was reduced to a level that caused the upper portion of the bag to sag, so that it wasn't high enough for them to use to get back out of the top of the barrel. A thief caught in his own trap! There is probably a really good lesson in life that could be expounded on from that, but . . .

As I kept an eye on the eagle, Nimrod was eyeing the otters. It was too much for him and he jumped into the water and gave chase. I watched in amusement as Nimrod paddled futilely after the otters, then I became concerned. He was extremely quick on land, but he was still small, and the eagle apparently thought he would make a great meal for her hungry eaglets waiting back at the nest, high on a cliff or in a lofty treetop. I had seen an eagle swoop down on him at breakneck speed a couple of times before, but Nimrod had always dodged them at the last second.

This time was different. Nimrod was in the water chasing the otters and distracted. He was no match for them, but he didn't know that and was focused on an otter swimming leisurely along, a safe distance from him. In the water, Nimrod was vulnerable. He was a clumsy swimmer and could not use his quickness.

I became alarmed when I saw the eagle circle and sure enough, close its wings and dive toward Nimrod at blistering speed. As the eagle descended in a tight, spiraling dive, Nimrod was completely unaware of the danger he was in. I was frantic. What could I do?

Things were happening so fast that even if I had come up with a plan, it would have been too late. Within mere seconds, the eagle was gliding expertly over the surface of the water behind the dog-paddling pooch, those long, black talons fully extended and an instant away from latching onto Nimrod's back and neck. I had risen from the chair fully intending to yell, but for some reason my mouth fell open and I was speechless. I guess I knew Nimrod was a goner.

I wondered if he would be able to twist and maybe bite the legs of the eagle as he was being lifted out of the water. I was certain he would not give up without a fight. I was appalled at the thought that the eagle might carry him high into the air, and if Nimrod was still struggling, simply drop him from a thousand feet or more and send him crashing onto the rocks below.

I was transfixed and simply stared at this mighty bird focused intently on snatching Kelly's dog. It was as if I had tunnel vision. I could only see those talons and Nimrod. Everything else was a blur. I could not even hear anything. It was as if I was at a silent horror show watching a mythological creature descending from the heavens, with a vengeance, on the little mighty warrior.

Was Nimrod going to be a bloody meal for this eagle and her brood? Everything was going in slow motion. How could my mind have so many thoughts racing through it in so little time? Then I saw the impossible.

Because the eagle had to come in on a shallow path, and due to her wide wings being used at the last minute to flap and slow her speed, Nimrod had somehow, incredibly, sensed her presence. Maybe he caught the moving shadow on the water, or possibly he heard the whooshing of the eagle's 7,000 feathers. I don't know.

I do know that I saw Nimrod instantly dive sideways and propel himself down into the water, furiously splashing water everywhere, distracting and causing the eagle to just barely graze him with those razor-like talons. Amazingly, the eagle's talons had failed to puncture Nimrod's hide and get a grip into his flesh.

The eagle fluttered, faltered for a second and then soared off empty-clawed. I just stood there stunned, and realized after a moment that I had not been breathing. Then the truth hit me. Nimrod was safe! I let out a long, slow breath of air and mentally said a heartfelt prayer of thanks that Nimrod's life had been spared.

I watched him as he paddled happily toward me. He reached the bank and trotted beside me, and wagging his slender body, shaking off water in a hail of droplets. He just wanted to be petted, nothing more. Or maybe he wanted to say, "Pretty cool move, huh, Dad?"

Nimrod wasn't making a big deal of his brush with death. He had no idea what a narrow escape he'd had or what a fearful fate he had avoided. Maybe that was for the best. Isn't it great how carefree animals appear to be and how little they seem to fret or care about danger or the future? They simply live each moment to the fullest.

I have seen men shake hands with death and others get paged. I have come to grips with my own mortality more than once. The wilds of Alaska certainly teach you to enjoy each minute you live, since it may be your last. It gives you pause to reflect on what your true priorities need to be. I can tell you this: Watching Nimrod survive spoke deeply to my heart that day.

Chapter 11 – The Call

Franklin Graham and our Grizzly Camp.

Chapter Eleven

The Call

"Creation is a special gift."

I have learned the hard way that you must be very careful with whom you make friends. Not necessarily the casual friends, but in particular those with whom you become close. I sincerely prayed to find a friend with whom I would enjoy golfing. God sent me a guy named Dave Eline, who is a plumber. I asked God a little dubiously, "Is Dave your choice for me as my new friend?" God wisely pointed out to me that my house was almost 50 years old, and the best friend I could possibly have would be a good plumber!

Actually, the best possible friends, could be a guide and a plumber. Dave has re-plumbed my entire house! I've enjoyed great golf at Granite Bay Country Club with him and he has loved his fishing trips at my Holitna lodge in Alaska.

There was a 2,000-member church, which was filled to overflowing capacity one Sunday morning. The preacher was ready to start the sermon when two men, dressed in long black coats and black hats, entered through the back door of the church. One of the two men walked to the middle of the church while the other stayed at the back. Both then reached under their coats and withdrew automatic weapons.

The man in the middle of the church announced, "Everyone willing to take a bullet for Jesus, stay in your seats!" Naturally, the pews emptied, followed by the choir. The deacons ran out the door, followed by the choir director and the assistant pastor. After a few moments, there were about twenty nervous people left sitting in the church. The preacher was gripping the pulpit tightly but holding steady.

The men put their weapons away and said gently to the preacher, "All right, pastor, the hypocrites are gone now. You may begin the service." (jokes.christiansunite.com)

The point is well made, but thankfully, there are exceptions. Some are the real McCoy. I remember hunting moose when I was very young with our wonderful Uncle Joe. We usually hunted in the early morning when the light was dim or in the evening when the sun was sinking. We would scan the horizon and the marshy fields for a bull moose. So often, a blackened stump in the distance would seem to move in the flickering light, and I would stare and strain my eyes to determine if it was a moose or a stump. I didn't own a good pair of binoculars then. I would ask Dad to use his scratched-up pair to check out the "stump." After doing this several times, Uncle Joe said, "Rock, you may get fooled into thinking a stump is a moose, but you will never spot a real moose and think it is a stump."

That is exactly what I have discovered about someone who is the authentic article in the church. The pretenders may fool many of us for a time into thinking they are what they proclaim. However, the ones whose lives match their lips are a special treat and a real joy to know. They are not perfect, but they also are not stumps and will never be mistaken as one.

So when I had the honor of meeting world-renowned evangelist Franklin Graham, son of the incomparable and godly Billy Graham, I was naturally cautious. Fame and heritage don't necessarily go hand in hand with a righteous life. Moreover, fame, with its attendant benefits, can often corrupt. Years ago, Franklin heard of me and came to the lodge for a week of fishing. He brought his wife Jane and his kids, Will, Ed, Roy and his beautiful daughter Sissy. Roy later became a lead guide for me, and Sissy washed many dishes with the girls. Let me tell you this, if you want to see what a man is really like, spend some time with him and his family or spend some time in the wilds on a fishing boat with him. The layers peel off and you will see what he is truly made of.

Franklin immediately fell in love with my family and the Alaskan wilds, and I with him and his family. He was no phony and we hit it off right from the outset. Franklin became so caught up in the Alaskan culture that he purchased several lots near mine and set up a Christian retreat that is a terrific place for adults and youth to go for restoration. He owns a Super Cub and is a fine pilot. He has come alongside many Alaskan Native causes, spending time, money and resources, when famine or other disasters have struck, to help Russian and Alaskan Native villages. Samaritan's Purse, which he promotes, rebuilt a village that experienced a devastating fire. Sometimes this has involved dangerous flying for these missions of support. His ministry and invaluable contributions have made a big difference in Alaska.

Over time, my view of Franklin has only increased, and we have hunted and fished often. This story is about a grizzly hunting trip we went on recently. In my first book, *Wild Men, Wild Alaska*, I wrote about the story of Franklin going after the now famous mammoth trophy moose, "Roscoe," that got the best of him, others and me over the years. Recently, in the same meadow, I have seen a huge moose that must be his son. Old Roscoe has been replaced by Junior Roscoe; and so go we all. Maybe Senior Roscoe died of old age and went to "moose heaven." After all, who could resist the call of Preacher Franklin Graham!

Franklin would often fly in for a day or two with some of his like-minded friends to fish and visit us at our lodge. Ironically, his birthday and that of my oldest daughter is on the same day. Somehow, he seemed to manage to come and celebrate with her and us on that day. He would discreetly slip her a one hundred dollar bill each year as her gift.

We had been inundated with grizzlies in our region, and they were wreaking havoc on the wild game. They were killing moose calves, young moose and even grown moose as well as caribou and myriads of other small animals. The grizzlies are not diminishing in population because there are always plenty of fish and berries to eat, and they are voracious predators and love killing wild game for food and, yes, sometimes just for sport. Because wolves and bears have outstanding predatory skills, and prey on caribou and moose passionately, the caribou and moose herds have been disappearing fast. The wild predators kill far more than hunters do. I had privately been asked by some authorities to target more predator animals for that precise reason.

The natural balance of nature is not served when the predators are flourishing and the rest of the animals are being destroyed en masse. When I see stickers or T-shirts calling for the preservation and "no hunting" of predator wolves, I ask myself, *How many species do we want to destroy in order to save this one animal?* And it is more than one animal; the beloved wolves and grizzlies are killing machines that destroy foxes, weasels, marten, beavers, mink, otters, caribou, moose, upland birds and on the list goes.

I mentioned this to Franklin and another longtime friend and pilot, Ralph Meloon, so the three of us decided to go grizzly hunting. I have written about "calling" in grizzlies before and felt confident that I knew of a location where I could do that for them. This particular call is done with a mouth instrument which, when blown into properly, imitates the terrifying screams of a bear cub being killed by a male grizzly (a boar). Boar grizzlies will often try to kill cubs simply so that the sow (mama grizzly) will go into heat sooner. Talk about a dysfunctional family!

There are some awesome videos of sows protecting their cubs against boar grizzlies. I guess bears are not the only families that get into fights over their kids, and usually big mama wins those fights. That sounds familiar.

Being full of snap, as usual, I confidently told Franklin and Ralph that I could "call" in a grizzly. I said that I had just the place in mind, about a hundred miles north of the lodge. It was next to the river, where the hillsides were full of berries and the river afforded sloughs (backwater inlets with little current) in which spawning salmon were plentiful. They both looked at me as if I was trying to sell them beach property at the North Pole. I shrugged and said, "So you don't believe in miracles, eh? O ye of little faith!"

We set off, each of us in our own plane. I brought along a guide, Adrian Parker, and our pilot landed us on a sand/gravel bar (a natural lengthy sandy, light gravel area created on the bends of winding streams and rivers) at the location I had scouted out previously. These gravel bars are often used to land bush planes in Alaska. The dangers can be quite severe as the sand can be mushy, the water may encroach on the strip and rocks can turn out to be much bigger than they appear from the air. The clearance needed for approach and take-off is curtailed due to heavy brush and trees and complicated by swirling winds. Most aren't long enough or level enough or don't have enough space, but a few are suitable. In the wilds, places to land an aircraft are precious and hard to find, so sand bars are a welcome, albeit tricky, place to use.

All three experienced pilots landed safely, though, and the work of setting up camp began. Tension was in the air because bear signs, scat (bear excrement), paw prints and half-eaten fish carcasses were everywhere. We were in bear heaven. I was mulling over some smart remark to make about bears and the hereafter to Franklin when I noticed him and Ralph pulling out some type of metal contraption from their planes.

Now, mind you, I had already begun the grunt work of putting up tents for all of us, setting up tables, chairs, cooking implements, water, and coolers and storing sleeping bags and gear. Most of the time, I get eager help from the guests— most of the time! But not today, no, sir. What were the esteemed guests doing while I was slaving away for them? That metal contraption turned out to be an electrically charged fence they wanted to put around their planes, which they had parked close together for that purpose.

I was thinking, *Why an electrically energized fence?* And hearing the reply, *Don't you know, Rocky? To keep the bears out, of course.* Honestly, I didn't really believe that puny fence, even if "charged," would deter any real grizzlies, but if it could, then why in the dickens would they just put it around their planes? Obviously, the planes were more important than any of us were!

While contemplating how the fence would be charged, I said sarcastically to Franklin, "We are way out here in the remote Alaskan wilderness. Where is your power source? You gonna plug it into the 'river current?' "

He shook his head disdainfully and said, "O ye of little faith! I will use power from above." Well, the power from above turned out to be a couple of big batteries they had brought. So, a scrawny metal fence charged by batteries was being trusted to keep mean interior wild grizzly bears away from their precious bush planes. I noticed sheepishly that *my* plane wasn't included in that protection. This was getting better by the minute.

Of course, you know what happened. I just didn't believe that lightweight three-wire fence would harm a butterfly, so I walked over to it and yep, I touched it—when the power was on. Holy Jehoshaphat! That thing knocked me on my butt. It was unbelievable how much energy that stinking thing put out. My faith in that fence was ratcheted up big time.

I always set up my personal tent far away from the guests' tents. Is this because I don't like them? No, that is not it at all. It is because my wife accuses me of snoring louder than a Harley bike with a busted muffler. She tried to tape record me one night. The speakers on the recorder blew out. One of the common themes at any men's camp the next morning is that each one accuses the other person of being the loudest "baddest" snorers in the camp. It is an argument I consistently lose, but only because all the other campers gang up on me. How fair is that?

One camper lamented to me that his snoring had destroyed his life. I immediately felt empathy and compassion for him and asked him if his wife had left him over his snoring. He said that he had never been married. That puzzled me and I asked him why his snoring had so badly affected him. He looked at me, shook his head sadly and said, "I like to sleep at work and it has cost me five good jobs!"

I bade everyone a good night and took the little one-man tent down to the end of the gravel bar, where the water was lapping up against the gravel and making a soothing splashing sound. I had just purchased this fancy tent and it was supposed to be easy, quick and warm, just perfect for one person. It measured 91 inches long and 36 inches wide—seemed like plenty of room, right? Over seven feet by three feet should be ample room for me. Wrong, very wrong. I had forgotten that it was a linear measurement. The tent had to fit *around* my body.

What is that, maybe four or five feet? Once I somehow managed to twist my hefty body into that tent, it was stretched over me like a Glad bag holding an oversized sandwich. I couldn't move without moving the entire tent. I tried to pull a rifle in with me, but the only position I could manage was holding it pointed skyward. I was unable to twist the rifle more than a few inches either way.

I had to leave the door open for the rifle and to provide as much room as possible. I could see outside and even though it was 10 p.m., it wasn't pitch-black dark. There was a light rain and this really complicated matters because I was getting wet. I was also getting angry. How had I spent so much money on a tent that I couldn't even fit into? I was an experienced long-time Alaskan guide, wasn't I? This was insane. Then the insanity multiplied. Straight away, I saw a huge grizzly sow and her cub enter into the river directly adjacent to me. They were only 40 yards away! I felt like a human sandwich wrapped up in a see-through plastic bag, a dandy grizzly dinner for mama and her kid.

I didn't want to attract their attention. I couldn't move and I couldn't even position the gun properly to protect myself. Was I becoming senile? How could this happen? I must tell you that I felt stupid. I lay there very still and watched mama and kid splashing in the river going after salmon. I saw the sow look my way curiously a few times and sniff the air. Each time I held my breath and froze. Hey, lady, I got no beef with you or your kid. I just don't want to be your dessert, okay? Where was that electrical fence when I needed it?

They were in no hurry and I was trapped. After awhile I relaxed a little because the sow didn't seem too concerned about the weird, green, lumpy-shaped human-smelling thing on the sand bar. And I needed rest. I had a grueling day planned for tomorrow. It appeared the bears were not going anywhere, so I tentatively shut my eyes, tried to wriggle quietly into a comfortable spot and summoned sleep. Yeah, right, no problem. I slept soundly—for about 30 seconds.

I had just read of a woman in the Porcupine Range who had a grizzly bite her head through the canvas tent wall, so my thoughts weren't very positive. This went on for several hours until at last I began to sleep in longer spurts, but I would awaken abruptly with visions of a big mouth full of grizzly teeth chomping into the tent.

Somewhere in the middle of the night, I thought either the bears moved on or maybe the snoring scared them. I wasn't sure, but the reality was that I couldn't see them and that was not really a comfort. The window of sight wasn't that large. Were they just outside the tent to the left or right? How close were they? How close would they be before I could hear them? Had they eaten enough salmon so that they weren't hungry for anything new?

This was nerve-racking. It was one of the most difficult nights I have ever spent in the wilderness. I realize some so-called "Grizzly Man" slept near bears for years, but eventually he was mauled to death by one, so those weren't comforting thoughts either.

At least I was very thankful for one thing. My good buddy Franklin's plane was safe. Just peachy! Where was my energized protection?

I certainly needed no alarm that morning. I was awake early and cautiously peering out of the "tent-bag" in every direction. I saw no unwanted visitors, so I got up and began to fix some fine grub for the guests and myself. That consisted of an all-time favorite, fried Spam and blueberry muffins. You haven't lived until you partake of that delicacy. Accompanied by natural oatmeal and campfire coffee, now that is a feast for royalty. Franklin and Ralph heartily approved.

We quickly donned our mega camouflage outfits, grabbed our rifles, got into a large rubber raft, then crossed the river to the side where a major slough was located almost directly across from where I had slept. At the far end of this large slough was a small creek that fed into it and into the river at large. This was a prime spot for the spawning salmon, and hundreds were swimming slowly back and forth. Many had already spawned, their bodies gleaming bright red. They were slowly dying and their death would provide food for myriads of creatures up and down the river system. These spent salmon were easy targets for all of the predators that sought them, including the grizzlies.

We exited, pulled our raft up onto the bank and then slowly waded up the slough along the shallow edge to the right. I knew that the splashing noises we made would simulate bear fishing in the water and would not alarm any grizzlies that might be nearby. As I looked around, I could see bear scat, fish remains, matted areas in the grass, lots of bear tracks and even torn-up areas where bears probably had fought over prime fish or fishing places. On the left side of the slough was a sloping embankment that went up fairly sharply for about 20 yards then leveled off into a gentler slope, which was covered in thick tundra.

I knew that higher up, the hill was loaded with blueberries. The rolling terrain was dotted with small black spruce trees. Near the water were scattered masses of alders on both sides of the slough. This backwater was not far from the main river, which was to our right. A small creek at the upper end of the slough fed into it and created a mild current toward the main river. It was idyllic. We were smack dab in the middle of bear country.

It was also beautiful. Many sloughs stink from stagnant water, muddy dirt bottoms, decaying fish and debris and are the breeding grounds of mosquitoes, numerous insects, algae and associated organisms. The mild current at this spot washed away and limited some of that, and the fall colors in the brush, trees and alders cast a beautiful golden hue over the slough, which was shimmering with the reddish color of the sluggish salmon. It was a snapshot in the cycle of life.

Our camouflage clothing blended perfectly into the green and browning foliage. When wearing camouflage apparel, I sometimes feel like I am being swallowed up by nature—that I am becoming one with Creation. It is a neat feeling. We all trudged along for a few moments soaking up all of this when all at once Franklin snorted, "When you gonna call up that grizzly, Rockstar?"

Franklin and Ralph were on my left and Adrian on my right. I glanced sideways to my left at Franklin and thought I could see a big smirk on both his and Ralph's faces. I quickly looked to my right at the guide, Adrian, and he was looking straight ahead, pretending he hadn't heard anything. I had seen that sow last night with her cub so I knew a bear call would work. Okay, boys, Rockstar was going into action!

I pulled out the trusty predator bear call (the one that simulates the screams of a cub being killed by a boar), put it to my lips, took a deep breath and began working it hard, with my mouth and cheeks puffing and filling with air. The sound is reminiscent of a combination of eerie screams, screeches, squeals and wails you might hear in a horror movie. I think if I were alone in the dark and unexpectedly heard these cries, I might faint. Well, I was going at it hard, swaying and blowing for all I was worth. My eyes were partially closed because I was concentrating on putting out the right sounds, terrifying sounds that I have actually heard in the wild.

Did I hear guffawing on my left? I opened my eyes and saw Franklin and Ralph, their free hands clasped over their mouths. Were they just nervous or were they trying not to laugh? They were looking at me in disbelief, shaking their heads and getting a big kick out of my antics. I made a face at them, took another huge breath and continued the bear calls. The more I worked it, the more I thought I could hear laughter. The four of us continued up the slough, my partners hooting and hollering and me wailing and screeching.

In due course, as we neared the end of the slough, we stopped and Franklin sat down for a minute. He seemed to be enjoying the crisp fall morning. I couldn't tell if the "loon" they were referring to was directed at me or to the river loon floating by, but I had a good idea. Their expressions eloquently said, "How could we possibly get close to a grizzly with that idiotic racket Rocky is making?" I gave the call one last series of my best sounds. And then it happened, I saw two brown flashes of fur about 60 or 70 yards up the hill on my left.

I pointed at the two grizzlies charging straight down the slope at us and screamed at Franklin, "There are two grizzlies headed straight for us! Shoot! Shoot! Now! Quick! Fire! Shoot!" Both Ralph and Franklin whirled toward the bears, quickly cocked their guns, put them in firing mode and aimed at the grizzlies headed down the hill at us. Ralph fired and neither of the bears missed a beat, but kept on coming. I looked at Franklin. He had calmly gotten down on one knee and was aiming at the grizzly on the right, but he hadn't fired. What was he waiting for? Had he gotten down on his knees to pray? "Shoot, Franklin, shoot!" I screamed again.

The grizzlies were closing fast and I was getting plenty worried. It is bad enough when one grizzly charges you, but to have two moving targets zigging and zagging down a hill to avoid the few spruce trees, yet still coming right at you, was very disconcerting. I wasn't sure how good a shot either man was. Believe me, they weren't laughing anymore. The grizzlies were not trophy size but were still big and strong, their muscles rippling under their fur as they kept flying down the hill looking intently at us. My mind was racing. This was starting to get serious. Come on, boys. SHOOT!

The bears were gorgeous, their fur was beautiful and healthy and they showed amazing agility as they were coming downhill at a run. Have you ever tried running down a sloped embankment? It is tricky to keep your balance on even ground, much less on soft, spongy, uneven terrain filled with obstacles and you're carrying hundreds of pounds. Even in the midst of horror-filled moments, I have noticed that my mind and the activity seem to slow in pace and my senses become more acute. I have been told similar stories from people as they watch a car spin out and head at them at high speeds, that they remember almost insignificant stuff in the midst of all the pandemonium.

Often people in life threatening situations hyper-focus on only one or two things. A gunshot victim may tell the officer how big the barrel was, or give a description of scratches on the gun handle or the color of the front sights and not even recall much about the suspect. Their entire mind is consumed with the object of destruction and little else.

My mind was consumed with these two big bears hauling down the hill at us. Why hadn't the guests shot them yet? I yelled again, "Shoot, shoot, shoot!" It was as if by saying the word "shoot" repeatedly it might magically cause their rifles to fire quickly and accurately. Still the bears kept coming, but I noticed, thankfully, that they were slowing down, or was it just my perception that they were easing their pace? I looked closely and sure enough, as they got to the last steep embankment, they were slowing. However, they were only about 30 yards away. If they wanted to put it into high gear again, we would have mere seconds to respond. This was getting critical. Should I shoot? I knew I could only do that if my life was in immediate peril, and although I might feel that way at that moment, I seriously doubted that I could convince an Alaskan court to see it the same way, especially when two experienced hunters were beside me with big guns trained on the oncoming beasts.

I then noticed that Franklin had yet to fire! Just how close did they need to be for him to blast away? Was he that cool under fire? Ralph had fired, but because of the commotion and yelling, I wasn't sure how many times he had pulled the trigger. I was sure of one thing: neither bear seemed the slightest bit concerned or injured.

I put my rifle on fire and held it tightly, ready to swing into action if those bears made the water line and started to cross. The water at this location came mostly from the creek that fed the slough, and the far side was a mere ten yards away. I think it was about a foot deep on average. It might look like an obstacle, but it would present absolutely no deterrent to these agile and vicious animals. These bears could traverse that ten yards so fast there would be very little chance for the shallow water to effectively slow them down.

The bears paused briefly at the top of the last 20-yard incline and seemed puzzled at what they were seeing. They had expected to find another boar grizzly killing a cub, but these strange objects in green and brown outfits certainly weren't that. "Shoot, guys, shoot!" I yelled again. This was a perfect opportunity. Still no shots rang out. Were the hunters trying to get a head shot? Were they trying to be too careful? Were they paralyzed? Then the bears started down the last incline. My heart was already pounding and I readied myself for a likely fight to the death.

Both bears reached the bottom of the incline and were now at the far edge of the slough, a scant ten yards away. I started to swing my rifle into action when I heard Franklin fire. Boom! I saw the bear on the right go down and quickly get up and start back up the hill. Boom! The bear went down hard and stayed down. This shot was a fatal one and the bear died quickly. The other bear hesitated when Franklin's first shot rang out. He spun on his heels and raced back up the incline, dirt from his rear paws flying everywhere. At the top, just before he would have reached level ground and likely have sped away untouched, I heard another shot. Bang! That bear went down immediately and died on the spot as well. Each bear had been killed, almost instantly, and neither suffered pain. I am always grateful for that.

What I was especially thankful for was that my buddies had come through at last. However, the delay and the sensation of how close these bears had come to being right on top of us, and probably killing one or two of us, had sent a rush of adrenaline straight through my body.

I began to relax when I realized that the bears weren't going to get up, and then I began to shake. I just stood there trying to keep my body steady, but I continued to shake. I reached into my pocket and got a Swisher Sweet cigar, lit it up, took a long soothing drag, then barked at Franklin. "If there ever was a time to smoke, Franklin, this is it. You better have a smoke!"

He exploded, "Rocky, you know I don't smoke! Put those things away. This is no time for a cigar!"

I started to reply when Ralph turned toward Franklin, grinned and said, "Franklin, there is a time and place for everything, and this is the time and place for a cigar!"

We all began to laugh and it was a special moment. We had faced a life-threatening situation, and our laughter served to relieve the tension that had built up. Ralph and I did smoke a cigar, but although we teased Franklin, we never did convince him to join us.

I often feel like a coach who watches his team in action trying to overcome the other team. The coach feels helpless and can't do anything but hope his team performs and comes through. That is how I felt watching this traumatic event unfold. It was a huge relief when the team came through. What a terrific bonding moment for three friends.

We flew the grizzlies back to the lodge, and as we were making our approach, Sharon and one of our daughters, came running out to meet us. Since we were back so early in the day, they were sure something had gone terribly wrong. There was no way we could have gotten two grizzlies this quickly. They watched anxiously as the three planes landed. They were amazed and happy when they learned the truth.

When we placed Franklin's grizzly on the ground at the lodge, our daughter was so happy for him that she started doing her imitation of an Indian victory war dance. We were all very thrilled for Franklin because he rarely has time to hunt seriously.

I sat outside with Franklin and we looked at the beautiful river, gazed at the mountains and Alaska's magnificent nature with all its fall colors weaving back and forth along the hillsides, and we had a great chat. I showed him the predator bear call and told him that a guy in Mississippi named Will Primos made all types of these calls for all kinds of creatures, and he is one of the best in the world at replicating the various sounds animals make, from ducks, deer, alligators, moose, elk, turkeys and a host of other animals.

I said, "Franklin, when you observe nature and see the incredible beauty and design from the air while flying, and on the ground when you walk these mountains, hills and valleys, does it still touch you and give you pause why anyone would think there isn't a Master Designer behind it all?"

He said, "Rock, you and I have talked about this before, and we both believe that God calls us in a couple of ways, that God knows the pulse of our hearts and the needs of our lives, and He created nature and this wonderful world as a gift to us. He wants us to appreciate His Creation, but more importantly, He wants us to appreciate and worship the Creator behind the Creation. He tells us in the Bible that man can examine the wonders of the earth and heavens and is therefore without an excuse not to believe there is God."

As a grizzled, older Alaskan guide, I have spent a lot of time contemplating animals and witnessing the majesty of the Last Frontier. You know, tree-stand thinking time. I believe there are two Bibles, both inspired by the same God. One is the orb we call planet Earth, which is God's open book to all people, nations and tribes that inhabit our planet. The earth and the universe sing out, shout out, that "I" as God am the Planner, Designer and Architect of all you see, touch and use. Your water, air, plants, fruit, meat, fish, clothing and comforts come from the good hand of God, to all people. He is saying, "Be good caretakers because with love I am entrusting to you this marvelous gift, planet Earth."

Franklin and I also agree that there is a second call made by God. It is a call to turn from our sins and acknowledge His shed blood for each of us. That is why God gave us the one perfect sacrifice, His sinless Son, Jesus, to die for our sins so that we could answer His second call. This is a very personal and intimate call to you, to confess your sins and accept Jesus so that you are seen as pure and forgiven by God, and can thus enjoy His creation and understand His personal call on your life. He wants to love us, be loved by us and be our Father forever.

I have stood at the precipice of the Grand Canyon and the astounding wonder of it moved me deeply. I have been unnerved by holding our precious newborns in my arms. I have seen many majestic sights, in Alaska and throughout the world, and some have caused me to worship with the intensity of their beauty. These were created by our Creator for us and they deeply affect us, because it reflects Him to us. Can you imagine being in the actual presence of that Creator for eternity? I cannot imagine living a life that doesn't show how grateful I am for the universal display of God's attributes, or that doesn't reflect how thankful I am for His Son's sacrifice and gift of eternal life.

Tight Lines, Straight Shots

Rocky

Note: *We need help. If these stories have resonated with you and you sense they would impact a son, daughter, father, mother, friend or anyone else who loves adventure, then please give the book to them. Buy 10 and share! Write a review on Amazon! Suggest tag search terms and click 'yes' on reviews you feel are helpful. We want to get the book's message to at least a million people. We believe America needs it and that it will impact lives positively.*

We have gotten incredible feedback from our first book, **"Wild Men, Wild Alaska."** *Scores of men, women, boys and girls have recounted life-changing results. I will make this offer. Go to www.alaskan-adventures.com and order both books from me. For $30, plus shipping, I'll sign them and send to whomever you designate. (The first edition will be hardcover; the sequel* **"Wild Men, Wild Alaska II"** *is only available in paperback.)*

What to Bring to Alaska on Your Trip!

*What to take on your Alaskan Hunting and Fishing Adventure of a lifetime. **Cabelas** stores caries most of these items or similar.*

Bonding in the Wild! If you don't believe that wilderness adventures can bring a family together, just ask the Hadley group. What a wonderful story of restoration.

This is what it is all about!

- ■ **Fishing: Guided**
    - ■ **Comfortable warm pants: 2-3 pair**
    - ■ **3 warm long sleeve shirts; 1-2 short sleeve shirts**
    - ■ **Tennis shoes and walking boots/shoes**
    - ■ **Wool socks/heavy duty**
    - ■ **Light thermal underwear**
    - ■ **Warm jacket/sweaters**
    - ■ **Personal toilet articles**
    - ■ **Mosquito repellent (Cutters is good) (May want net)**
    - ■ **Hat/glasses/light gloves**
    - ■ **Camera/film w/ case**
    - ■ **All weather rain gear**
    - ■ **Fishing Pliers *(A MUST)**

■ **Polarized Fishing Glasses**

■ **Alaskan-Adventures has ALL the equipment you will need, although you are welcome to bring any fishing gear you like. We have ultra-light, medium and heavy-duty rods, lures, line, etc. and we have a fully stocked tackle shop. (We do not provide/sell fly-fishing gear, or odd size waders (we have sizes 9-13 only). We don't provide raingear.**

■ **Gift Shop/Tackle Shop Alaskan-Adventures does have a fully equipped Tackle Shop, (no fly-fishing gear) and a Gift Shop. We sell great outdoor Shirts, T-Shirts and Sweat-shirts with the Alaskan-Adventures Logo, as well as other items.**

■ **Gratuities -- Staff Gratuities are not included in the price. The suggested amount is $100-$150 a week per fisherman**

■ **Fishing: Unguided**

　　■ **General Equipment List**

　　　　■ **Waders or Hip Boots**
　　　　■ **Good quality rain gear**
　　　　■ **Hat**
　　　　■ **Fingerless Gloves**
　　　　■ **Long Underwear (2 Sets)**
　　　　■ **Boot socks**
　　　　■ **Insect Repellent-Muskol, Space Shield, Shoo Bug Jacket (if bad insect area)**
　　　　■ **Waterproof Match Box**
　　　　■ **2 warm shirts**
　　　　■ **2 pairs of warm pants**
　　　　■ **Warm Jacket or sweater**
　　　　■ **Extra medical prescriptions (if applicable)**
　　　　■ **Knife**
　　　　■ **Camera/Film w/ case**
　　　　■ **Fishing** <u>license</u>
　　　　■ **Small Flashlight**
　　　　■ **Duffel bag**

　　Rod Tube. If your rod is not already in a durable, hard tube, we suggest buying a piece of PVC pipe at your local hardware store to carry it in.

　　■ **King Salmon**

　　　　■ **Casting Rod/Reel: Lamiglas G1318T or G1316T and Shimano TRN 200 G**

- Spinning Rod/Reel: Lamiglas G1319 and Penn 650 or 850SS
- Dai Riki Monofilament 30 or 36 lb. test or Maxima Monofilament 20 or 25 lb.
- Extra line
- Leader Wheels 46 lb. Dai Riki or 30 lb. Maxima
- Rosco Snap Swivels Size 5 or 7
- Pencil lead 1/4"
- Pixee 7/8 oz. Hammered Brass/Orange, Hammered Nickel/Red
- Spin-N-Glo Kits Size 2 or Size 0 Pink, Flame, Pearl/Red
- Hot Shot 025 Orange, Silver, Blue Pirate
- Magnum Tadpolly Nickel/Blue, Red, Nickel
- Magnum Wiggle Wart
- Krocodile 1 3/4 oz chartreuse or chrome
- Tee Spoon #5 and Skagit Special #6
- Vibrax Spinner Size 6 Silver, Silver/Red
- Mepps Giant Killer
- Single Siwash Hooks 3/0 4/0
- Hook File
- Lure Box
- Scissors or Clippers
- Polarized Fishing Glasses
- Long Nose Pliers
- Swiss Army Knife
- Fishing Vest or Hip Pack

- **Chums, Silvers, Sockeyes, Large Char, and Steelhead**
  - Casting Rod/Reel: Lamiglas G 1306T and Quantum 1420
  - Spinning Rod/Reel: Lamiglas G1307 and Penn 450SS
  - Dai Riki Monofilament 19 lb. test or Maxima Monofilament 12 lb. test
  - Extra line
  - Dai Riki Leader Wheels 15 and 19 test
  - Rosco Snap Swivels Size 10 and 7
  - Pixee 1/2 oz and 7/8 oz Silver/Red Silver/Green
  - Steelee 1/2 oz Metallic Green, HB/FL Stripe, HN/FL
  - Little Cleo 3/4 oz
  - Maribou Jigs 1/4 oz Red/White, Pink
  - Mepps Silver & Gold Size 5

What to Bring to Alaska on Your Trip of a Lifetime

- Roostertail 1/2 oz Flame
- Tee Spoon Size 4
- Vibrax size 5 Silver or Silver/Green
- Twist On Lead Strips and Split Shot
- Hook File
- Lure Box
- Scissors or Clippers
- Polarized Fishing Glasses
- Long Nose Pliers
- Swiss Army Knife
- Fishing Vest or Hip Pack
- Single Siwash Hooks 1/0, 2/0, 3/0

- **Rainbows, Char and Grayling**
  - Spinning Rod/Reel: Lamiglas G1212 and Penn 430SS
  - Dai-Riki Monofilament 12 test or Maxima 8 lb. test
  - Extra line
  - Leader Wheels 10 lb. test Dai Riki
  - Rosco Lock Snap Swivel Size 10
  - Pixie 1/2 oz Hammered Brass/Orange, and Hammered Nickel/Red
  - Steelee 1/2 oz HamBr/Fl Stripe, or HamNi/Fl Stripe
  - Maribou Jigs 1/4 oz Red /White, Black
  - Roostertail 1/8 oz and 1/4 oz Flame, White, or Yellow
  - Shyster Spinners Fire/Black Dot 1/3 oz
  - Mepps Spinners Silver or Gold Size 3
  - Vibrax Spinners Silver Size 3
  - Single Siwash Hooks Size 2 and 1/0
  - Single Egg Fly-Peachy King, Alaskan Roe, Baby Pink, & Salmon Egg Size 6
  - Twist On Lead Strips and split shot
  - Hook File
  - Lure Box Scissors or Clippers
  - Polarized Fishing Glasses
  - Long Nose Pliers
  - Swiss Army Knife Fishing Vest or Hip Pack

- **Fly-Fishing**
  - **Words of Wisdom... The first time Alaska fisherman will quickly find that it is a long way to the nearest tackle store up in Alaska. We suggest complete self-containment equipment-wise when you board the plane for your trip of a lifetime. Alaskan-Adventures does not sell/provide fly-fishing gear.**

- **King Salmon. (Fly-Fishing)**
    - Rod: Lamiglas G1298-9 or G1299-9
    - Reels: SA System II 1011 or 89
    - Extra Spool
    - Fly line backing 30 lb.
    - Teeny 300 and Wet Tip Lines
    - Tapered Leaders 16 and 20 lb. tippets
    - Dai Riki Leader Wheels .017 and .019
    - Twist On Lead & Split Shot
    - Hook File
    - Fly Box
    - Scissors or Clippers
    - Polarized Sun Glasses
    - Long Nose Pliers
    - Swiss Army Knife Fishing Vest
    - Outrageous 4/0
    - Crazy Charlie Purple Pearl 4/0
    - Polar Shrimp 1/0
    - Teny Nymph Size 2 Pink, Flame, Black, Ginger
    - Alaskabous, Pixees Revenge, Showgirl Size 1/0
    - Wiggle Tail Orange or Pink Size 1/0
- **Chums, Silvers, Sockeyes, Large Char and Steelhead. (Fly-Fishing)**
    - Rods: Lamiglas G1298-8
    - Reels: S.A. System II 78, PFlueger Medalist 1495 1/2 Hardy St. Aidan and Marguis 10
    - Extra spools
    - Fly Line Backing
    - Floating, Wet tip and T300 Teeny lines
    - Tapered Leaders 12 lb. Tippet
    - Dai Riki Leader Wheels .013 to .015
    - Twist on Lead Strips & Split Shot
    - Hook File
    - Fly Box
    - Scissors or Clippers
    - Polarized Fishing Glasses
    - Long Nose Pliers
    - Swiss Army Knife
    - Fishing Vest
    - Alaskan Bug Eyes Size 2
    - G String Size 2
    - Teeny Nymph Size 2 Pink, Flame, Black, Ginger
    - Babine Special Size 2 & 4

- **Skykomish Sunrise Size 2**
- **Bright Roe Pink Size 2**
- **Polar Shrimp Size 2 & 4**
- **Outrageous 1/0**
- **Alaskabous, Show Girl, Pixee Revenge, Coho Size 1/0**
- **Woolly Bugger Purple Size 2**
- **Rainbows, Char and Grayling. (Fly-Fishing)**
  - **Rods: Lamiglas G1297-6 or G1298-6**
  - **Reels: SA System II 67 PFlueger 1495 Hardy Princess Backing**
  - **Floating, Wet tip, and T200 Teeny Lines**
  - **Tapered leaders 6 and 8 lb. tippet**
  - **Dai Riki leader wheels .008, .009, .010, .011**
  - **Twist On lead strips & Split Shot**
  - **Strike indicators**
  - **Fly floatant**
  - **Line cleaner**
  - **Hook file**
  - **Fly box**
  - **Scissors or clippers**
  - **Polarized fishing glasses**
  - **Long nose pliers**
  - **Swiss Army Knife**
  - **Fishing Vest**
  - **Single Egg Flies Size 6 Peachy King, Alaskan Roe, Baby Pink, and Salmon Egg**
  - **Woolly Worms Size 2 & 4 Black/Black, and Grizzly/Black**
  - **Black Maribou Muddler Size 4**
  - **Black Matuka Size 2**
  - **Matuka Sculpin Size 2, Olive**
  - **Teeny Nymph Size 4 Pink, Flame, Black, Ginger**
  - **Black Maribou Leach Size 2**
  - **Mouserat**
  - **Wiggle Lemming**
  - **Babine Special Size 4, 6, and 8**
  - **Polar Shrimp Size 4**
  - **Bitch Creek Size 4 and 6**
  - **Girdle Bug Size 4**
  - **Woolly Bugger Size 2 and 4 Black**
  - **Muddler Minnow Size 4 and 6**
  - **Black Gnat Size 16 Grayling**
  - **Mosquito Size 16**
  - **Humpy Size 12**

- **Wulff Grizzly and Royal Size 10**
- **Bright Roe Orange Size 4**
- **Egg Sucking Leech Size 4 Purple and Black**
- Hunting: Guided
    - From the owner..."Think layers of warm waterproof clothing, not bulky heavy coats, etc. River and mountain hunting is cold. Your feet and hands are most important, so bring wool: no substitutes."
    - All gear, including rifle, should not weigh more than 50 lbs. per person. All flying is done in small aircraft and space and weight are at a premium. All clothing should be packed in soft-sided duffel canvas bags. Rifles should be in soft cases. Note: Soft cases for rifles are allowed on bush planes but not on most commercial flights. Regulations change frequently.
    - Warm heavy-duty waterproof Gortex rain gear. Raingear must be quiet and camouflage for successful trophy hunting. See Alaskan-Adventures.com Resources page for online outfitters and specific suggestions for both raingear and footwear.
    - 2-3 comfortable warm pants
    - 3-4 warm long sleeve shirts
    - Tennis shoes, walking boots, or hip boots (Schnee's 14" Arctic or Cabela's Guide boots are recommended).
    - Wool socks/heavy duty
    - Thermal underwear
    - Warm Jacket/Sweaters
    - Personal toilet articles
    - Mosquito repellent (Cutters is good)
    - Hat/glasses/warm Gortex gloves
    - Camera/Film
    - Ammo, Rifle
    - Some lures, mepps, etc. (Poles already there)
    - Fishing license if you plan to fish.
    - Binoculars (If you have them)
    - Game bags (A Must)
    - Skinning knives
    - License and tags for moose, caribou, grizzly/brown bear or black bear. Must have prior to arrival at hunting area! They cannot be shared between hunters.
- Hunting: Unguided
    - This is for an unguided Moose, Caribou and/or Black Bear Hunt with excellent fishing. The great

advantage of this location is a well-stocked remote private lodge, (great shelter) in a heavily populated game area. You can run this river system for hundreds of miles. It's beautiful water... unbelievable country! The list of the clothing/equipment to bring is much the same as the guided hunts except as noted below.

- Hunt/Fish Description: (Depending on Season)
    - Fish: King Salmon, Silver Salmon, Northern Pike, Sheefish, Grayling.
    - Hunt: Moose, Caribou, Black Bear (Cannot hunt other types of big game animals unguided per regulations).
    - Black Bear can be shot on a Caribou or Moose Tag. Any tag can be used for equal or lower value animal.
- Alaskan-Adventures currently provides the following when staying at the Holitna Lodge (subject to change without notice). Check www.Alaskan-Adventures.com for updated info:
    - Five sleeping cabins; one main lodge; sauna/shower cabin, generator, propane
    - Freezer
    - Kitchenware, eating utensils
    - Staples: Flour, sugar, salt, pepper, coffee, tea, cooking oil, beans, rice, and miscellaneous food and spices.
    - Twelve boats/motors-this includes 40 gallons of gas per party of four. (After that there is a charge per gallon, current AA rate, includes oil.)
    - Guide tents, sleeping bags-(however for those going on field trips, for personal comfort we suggest you bring your own) sleeping bag pads
    - Camp stoves, misc. camping gear (If you choose to camp upriver on an extended trip).
- Alaskan-Adventures DOES NOT pay for the following:
    - Hunting License/Tag-Must buy in Anchorage prior
    - Odd size Hip Boots (we provide sizes 9-13 only) Client responsible for all other sizes.
    - Rain Gear
    - Round-Trip Airfare to Anchorage, R/T Anchorage to Aniak/Holitna, R/T Red Dev-

il/Holitna unless such expenses are specifically agreed to by Alaskan-Adventures on a case by case basis, and these are usually via upgraded guided fishing or hunting packages.

- Cooks or any food or drinks not listed
- Any gas above the 40 gallon (per party of 4) limit. Extra gas, (includes oil) available at AA rate per gallon in force at time of use.
- Any overweight meat haul/or freight
- 35 or 75 lb. wax meat boxes
- Game bags, knives, saws, guns, ammo. Please purchase official Alaska Game Bags prior to your trip. Order online and have them sent to the Holitna Lodge - Alaskan-Adventures PO Box 90 Mile 36 Sleetmute, Alaska. We suggest the following bags: AMP7 Alaska Pack - 7-bag package that includes bags, tags and gloves. This will handle 2 Caribou or 1 moose. The MEC460 4 pack will handle one animal and the ATB3648 is great for cape/hide transportation.
- There is a $50.00 prop fee deposit on each boat used 25 HP and under and $100.00 prop fee deposit on each boat over 25 HP, various sizes are available.
- Caping or Packing of meat
- Medical or Personal Injury Insurance

About the Author

Rocky McElveen with his wife, Sharon, are owners of Alaskan Adventures. Rocky, the son of an Alaskan missionary and a seminary graduate, was raised in Alaska and knows Alaska's charm and challenges better than anyone. For over twenty years he has been a professional guide there. His knowledge of our last great frontier along with his warm, hospitable manner adds an unprecedented dimension to his credentials as a master fishing and registered hunting guide. He is esteemed as a friend by many: President George Bush, Sr., General Charles E. "Chuck" Yeager, MLB player Dave Dravecky, Bob Seiple – president of World Vision, Pastor Chuck Swindoll, Evangelist Franklin Graham and Oakland A's pitcher Mike Moore, to name only a few. Rocky is one engaging guy to be around!

Rocky has lived through the most harrowing experiences his profession has to offer. His masterful stories relate the courage and bonds that develop when facing death and tragedy together, yet which also bring a deep appreciation of our Creator. His stories are told with such wit, insight and intrigue that they make him stand far above the crowd.

His best-selling (in its class) first book, "Wild Men, Wild Alaska" is a must read. Rocky has been on national TV and Radio shows in the US and Canada. He is a nationally sought after speaker, hosting wild game dinners that are normally packed beyond capacity and a huge success. For info on booking Rocky, see www.rockymcelveen.com or www.alaskan-adventures.com or call: 1-800-392-6210.

10062529R00133

Made in the USA
San Bernardino, CA
05 April 2014